ONE OF THE WEST'S ALL-TIME GREATS IN COLLEGIATE BASKETBALL

Eleanor Olson

Elinor Olson

ELEANOR OLSON

COPYRIGHT © 1991 BY ELEANOR OLSON

ALL RIGHTS RESERVED.

PRINTED IN THE UNITED STATES OF AMERICA

BY PUBLISHER'S PRESS

SALT LAKE CITY, UTAH 84119 U. S. A.

ISBN 0-9628317-0-0

DEDICATED TO:

ZENA BETH CROCKETT

WHO INFLUENCED ME TO BECOME AN ENGLISH TEACHER

AUTHOR'S NOTE

Wayne impressed me the first time I saw him in a varsity game, January 5, 1963, against Brigham Young University. He was calm and in control, unrattled by the constant pressure. After watching him on and off the court, he became my personal hero. I was absolutely devastated by his tragic death.

I decided to write this book the first year I taught English when I read a quote by Benjamin Franklin that said, "If you would not be forgotten, as soon as you are dead and rotten, either write things worth reading, or do things worth the writing." I knew this was a way I could keep Wayne "alive" and repay him and his parents for his great example and friendship.

The English Department Chairperson at USU, Pat Gardner, encouraged me with this project as did my college freshman English teacher, Zena Beth Crockett. My family and friends, and Wayne's family and friends plus my students at Roy High have also given their support.

ACKNOWLEDGEMENTS

Love and appreciation go to my parents and my sister and brother Sally and Kim for their understanding of my hero-worship of Wayne while I was in college. They never teased or put me down because I put Wayne on a pedestal. Their belief in my abilities to write this book and encouragement when times were hard helped me to persevere.

I express deep thanks to those people who granted me interviews and shared their experiences with Wayne. Without Helen, Joe, and Ronnie Estes this book wouldn't have been possible. They not only shared their thoughts, feelings, and remembrances but also letters that people wrote to them at the time of Wayne's death, newspaper clippings they had saved during his high school and college career, yearbooks, and personal letters that Wayne had written to them. They are now my dear friends. Jim Furaus, Judy Morstein Martz, John and Katherine Cheek, Charles Williams, Helen Divine, Mick Gee, Tom White, Pat Connors, Dexter Leonard, Tanna Nazer Bebo, and Elmer Carsone from his youth willing talked with me and shared much more than I could possibly use. LaDell Andersen, Evan Sorenson, Norvel Hansen, Lois Downs, Del Lyons, Mike Murry, Darnell Haney, Troy Collier, Mike Casey, Reid Goldsberry, Phil Johnson, Alan Parrish, Gary Watts, Hal Hale, Pete Ennenga, Doug Moon, Terry Cale DeRohan, Paula Bandy Jory, Donna Andersen, Brian Andersen, and Richard Wright from Wayne's USU days added greatly to my information.

I am also grateful to the sports writers from the *Logan Herald, Salt Lake Tribune, Deseret News, Student Life,* and *Anaconda Standard.* Because they recorded Wayne's athletic accomplishments in detail, I was able to document much of Wayne's life. Craig Hislop, USU Sports Information Director, helped with statistics and pictures.

I appreciate Leslie Cutler Stitt, my editor, who helped me stand back from the book and my feelings. Levi Peterson, Randy Hollis, Terry Sheffield, and Linda Evans also read early drafts of the book and gave encouragement. Brent Evans designed the cover and did the page set-up of the book.

TABLE OF CONTENTS

Author's Note vi
Acknowledgements vii
1. February 8, 1965 1
2. Beginnings of Greatness 19
3. Overcoming the Odds 25
4. The Glory Year 41
5. The New Recruit 53
6. The Varsity Team 67
7. Aiming High, 1963-1964 89
8. Top of the Heap 111
9. Legacy 135
10. Since then 141

CHAPTER 1
FEBRUARY 8, 1965

7:00 AM

The mercury had risen to a still-chilling 12 degrees F in Logan, Utah, when the alarm went off in Wayne Estes's bedroom. Instead of lumbering his six-foot six-inch, 225-pound frame to the bathroom like a bear coming out of hibernation as he usually did, he hustled to the shower thinking about the weekend and how it applied to his future. "If I set the fieldhouse record tonight, the Lakers might draft me. Hope Paula won't mind living in L.A. I should have talked to her about that." After eating breakfast and doing the dishes, he paced back and forth between the bedroom and the living room, with no premonition that not only would he play the last and best game of his life, but that he would never again repeat this morning's routine.

Wayne's usual pregame nervousness was more intense this day. Wanting to set the fieldhouse record that would also put him at 2,000 career points, he felt the day move in slow motion. In his Principles of Secondary Education class on the Utah State University campus, Dean John Carlisle handed back essay tests from the week before. It covered the purpose of education in relationship to the nature of society. Not particularly known for academic brilliance, Wayne grinned at the B+ on his paper, then compared grades with Del Lyons, his roommate and former teammate.

Wayne Estes: A Hero's Legacy

After class Dean Carlisle called Wayne back as he headed for the door, "Your paper had substantial quality. I'm glad you don't neglect your studies for basketball."

"Thanks, Dean," Wayne said, "but you don't have to worry about my studies. I'm going to graduate. I know I can't play basketball forever."

"But you do play tonight. I understand you're not far from the 2,000 point mark. I hope you make it."

"I'll sure do my best."

1:20 PM

Before the 1:30 classes, the yearbook sports editor passed Wayne and Del in Old Main, the original building on campus with block A's on all sides of the tower. An authority on all the sports stats, she interrupted them, "You played a great game Saturday, even if the Y did win. I sat with the Y student body, and they groaned every time you touched the ball."

"Thanks, El. Things should be better from here on out. I don't think we'll lose another one this season." As she started away, Wayne said, "Make sure you come to the game tonight."

"I wouldn't miss it—you'll be setting a record or two."

"You better love it even if I don't get the records."

After she left, Wayne voiced his concerns to Del. "Everyone is expecting me to get those records tonight. I want them too, but 46 points is a lot to expect. My stomach is churning already."

Del tried to ease the tension he felt building in Wayne, "You're always nervous before games. I guess that's what makes you so competitive. Loosen up. You'll do fine."

4:30 PM

While Wayne was eating the pre-game meal with his teammates, Mike Murry, a friend and teammate from Wayne's freshman year, arrived from Salt Lake City. They had arranged the night before to

February 8, 1965

meet outside the cafeteria after the pre-game meal and go to the game together. When Wayne finished, Mike introduced him to his friend, John Vassey, and they went to Wayne's apartment. They played darts for a while and talked about Westminster College, a small college in Salt Lake City, which Mike and John now attended, before Wayne started getting anxious to get to the fieldhouse. "Do you mind going up a little early?"

"Na, we can visit while you get ready and then watch the freshman game."

Del told them, "Go ahead now. I'll meet you a little later."

5:45 PM

After sitting in the stands for only a few minutes, Wayne left his friends and went to the dressing room. As he dressed in his uniform and warm-ups, he complained to Alan Parrish who lockered next to him, "My arms feel numb." To check things out, Alan punched him in the upper arms. Rubbing them, Wayne worried aloud, "I can't feel anything."

Coach LaDell Andersen, listening to Wayne worry and familiar with Wayne's pregame jitters, didn't want him to experience any more pressure. He reassured Wayne by saying, "It's just your nerves. It'll go away as soon as you get into the game."

8:00 PM

The contest with Denver University started off slowly. Both teams spent a lot of time controlling the ball (this was in the days before the shot clock), but neither team could hit many baskets. Wayne missed his first three or four shots. With ten minutes gone, Denver knotted the score 13–13. When Utah State had only made three buckets in twelve tries, Andersen called time-out. Huddling around Andersen, the team listened as Wayne again complained to Andersen, "My arms are numb; I can't hit anything. Maybe you better take me out."

Myron Long tried to help, "It's just jitters, Wayne."

Wayne Estes: A Hero's Legacy

"My jitters always go away after the opening tip. What if I've injured myself?" Wayne worried.

Wayne's lack of confidence made Andersen apprehensive. He had never seen Wayne not want to play. Hiding his concern, he told Wayne, "Go out and see what happens."

Within a minute, Wayne broke the Aggies out of their slump. Hitting six straight field goals with an assortment of jump shots, baseline hooks, and an occasional lay-up, he helped USU widen its lead to 27–19 with 4:30 left in the first half. Denver sagged three men on him, and he had to use every type of shot he possessed. Denver's six-foot-five senior, Jack England, had declared before the game, "I'll hold Estes down." He guarded Wayne as closely as possible but couldn't stop him.

As the Aggies increased their margin, the game became a Denver-Estes battle. Denver had jumped ahead early 13–5, but Wayne's shooting spree—seven of eight attempts in the last seven minutes—gave him the half-time advantage, 24–21 as USU led 39–21.

Walking to the dressing room for half-time, a puzzled Wayne talked to Parrish about the turn-around in his ability to hit everything he touched. "I don't know how they're going in," Wayne claimed. "I'm throwing them up, but someone else is putting them in."

Coach Andersen, worried about his star player, went over to where Wayne sat on the bench. "How's the numbness?"

"I still can't feel anything," Wayne insisted.

"Well, get another 24 points the second half, and we'll operate after the game," Andersen teased.

8:40 PM

The fieldhouse was electric the second half. The entire student body knew Wayne was after the magic 2,000 career-points. They counted down. His patented baseline hooks, a shot Denver couldn't stop, zeroed in with regularity. He interspersed those with pushers

February 8, 1965

and jumpers from the side, occasionally moving into the tight post to handle rebound buckets.

He didn't disappoint the 4,972 screaming fans in the Nelson Fieldhouse as he canned ten of thirteen shots in the final half in addition to pulling down fourteen rebounds.

When Wayne pulled within two points of the record, official score keepers passed the word to Andersen, but before he could call a time-out, Wayne had set the fieldhouse record. When the team huddled around Andersen, he told Wayne, "You need one basket to reach the 2,000-point milestone. You set the fieldhouse record with that last basket. Men, get him the ball and then we'll take him out."

Almost immediately, Wayne received the ball. He passed it back to LeRoy Walker, who made the basket. The next time down the court, Pete Ennenga passed him the ball. Wayne swung his left foot around and broke the 2,000 mark on a fifteen-foot baseline jumper with 4:44 on the scoreboard.

Wayne had just reached two goals, most points scored in the fieldhouse (48) and 2,001 career points. Bedlam broke out in the fieldhouse. Officials stopped the clock as teammates poured onto the court to congratulate the big, smiling 21-year-old senior for a job well done. After Manager Don Scudder presented Wayne the game ball, Andersen sat him down. Wayne quickly tucked his head to his hands. Andersen had to nudge him several times before he rose for a split second, acknowledging the wild ovation.

The fans chanted, "We want Estes! We want Estes!" But Wayne remained on the bench with his 48 points for the rest of the game. USU won 91–69.

9:20 PM

After the game the team hurried to the dressing room for their private celebration. Coach Andersen headed for the press box at the top of the fieldhouse to have his standard post-game interview with commentator Reid Andreasen from Logan's KVNU. Responding to a reporter's questions before he reached the stairs, Andersen described

Wayne Estes: A Hero's Legacy

Wayne, "There is a wonderful boy. There's no more conscientious man I know. Did you see him pass that ball back out when he only needed those two more points? There'll never be another like him."

Meanwhile, Wayne was accepting the pats and the congratulations of his teammates. "I can't believe it. And you guys kept passing me the ball. The record belongs to you too."

"Wayne," trainer Jim Railey shouted above the noise, "Andreasen wants you upstairs for the post-game interview in seven minutes."

"Be right there," Wayne called out and headed into the showers.

Following the five-minute news broadcast, Reid Andreasen started interviewing Coach Andersen. They made small talk in the press box before talking about Wayne and his records. Andersen was full of adulation, "No one could be prouder than I am. He's been tremendous. When he leaves us seven games from now and goes elsewhere, I know folks here will really miss him, the greatest scorer in Aggie history and one of the greatest scorers of all time in major collegiate basketball. Only fifteen or sixteen other men of major caliber universities have ever scored 2,000 points or more. And he's one of them.

"We couldn't be prouder of this guy, as you all know. His teammates all rushed onto the court after Wayne scored the 2,000 point and broke the fieldhouse record. They all have a great deal of respect for him. It's a tremendous tribute to a great, great player.

"The funny part of it was he came over and said his arms were all numb. And he went out and made five straight. At the half I asked him how they felt, and he said things hadn't changed. You see that's the tremendous touch he has. He had lots of pressure on him.

"When we told him during a time-out that he needed two points for the 2,000 mark and the fieldhouse record, he goes out and hits a real tough jump shot for the record. Now that's the kind of pressure-clutch shooter he is. Most guys you would tell them that, and they'd miss five or six before they'd finally bat one in. This guy takes a tough shot and breaks all the records. Everybody has enjoyed watching him.

February 8, 1965

Since we have four more home games to do this, the fans will come out in droves to see this guy perform."

Talking into the microphone, Andersen stared at the empty court. "Wayne should own all the records before he graduates. He's the greatest shooter we've ever had here and maybe one of the greatest of all time in any college. He fits that category."

As Andreasen followed Andersen's gaze, Wayne approached the booth. "Here comes Wayne now. Wayne, come on over here. I know many have already congratulated you, but I want to extend mine on a great effort. I know this makes you feel wonderful to know you've not only broken the fieldhouse record but reached that 2,000 mark."

Clearing his throat, Wayne looked at the microphone on the table, aware of the listening audience. "Thanks, Reid, it's about the greatest feeling I've ever had. Not just breaking the records but knowing all the team is behind me. If it wasn't for them, I'd never have gotten the shots I did get. I'm really proud to know they were behind me and all the people. That's just about the greatest feeling I've ever had."

Andreasen interrupted, "You've drawn the adoration of the fans here in the Nelson Fieldhouse tonight. Talking with Coach Andersen here a few minutes ago, he said when you started the ball game, you had numb arms. I'd like to see you numb all the time, boy."

"Yeah, it was kind of funny," Wayne responded. "My arms are still numb; I don't know why. I started out the game, as you know, missing the whole basket about three times. I said, 'Oh, oh, this is going to be a bad night.' Then I kind of forgot all about it. During the whole game my arms felt the same way. Some went in and some didn't."

"You had 24 at half and everyone here enjoyed watching you. You not only broke a great record, but I'm sure you're looking forward to possibly breaking a few others."

Without guile, Wayne admitted he was aware of the records, "Are there any others to break? We'd better look for them if there are."

Wayne Estes: A Hero's Legacy

"Wayne, I understand your folks will come down to witness the last game you'll play in the George Nelson Fieldhouse—six games away, right?" Andreasen asked.

"Yes, they'll come down for the last game."

"What are your feelings," Andreasen probed, "as the season starts drawing to a close as you attempt to leave Utah State and proceed on life's way, you might say?"

"I'd sure like to have a few more seasons to play. We should have won more ball games this year. I wish I had about two more seasons to play," Wayne said.

Andreasen followed with a barrage of questions. "Have you made any plans as you get ready to graduate? Have you had any pro offers or what would the pro ranks do with a guy your size? Would they put you in there on the forward line or make a guard out of you? Do you think you could play guard?"

Wayne, remembering his lack of offers after high school, expressed his insecurity, "That's what I'm worried about, Reid. I don't know where I'll play, if I do. I've had a few feelers, and I talked to the Los Angeles Laker coach. He told me I had a pretty good chance to play. I'll have to play it by ear, I guess."

Concluding the interview, Andreasen looked at Wayne. "All right, Wayne, I'd certainly like to see you play in a lot of games. Everywhere you go, I'll tell you one thing—after you leave Utah State, a lot of fans will follow your career, and we want to wish you a lot of luck. And thanks for coming up."

"Thanks, Reid."[1]

9:35 PM

As the clock on the fieldhouse wall ticked, other events had already been set in motion. About a mile from the fieldhouse, two cars loaded with students raced down Fourth North behind the girls' dorms

---

[1] Reid Andreasen, interview with LaDell Andersen and Wayne Estes, KVNU Radio, Logan, Utah, February 8, 1965.

February 8, 1965

and the library. The Ford lost control at eighty miles an hour and hit the center cement island as it skidded rounding the curve. The car spun 180 degrees, smacked a Pontiac stopped on College Boulevard and Fourth North, and rammed into the light pole. The police arrived shortly and began working with the ambulance crew to remove three injured students from the Ford.

9:45 PM

After the interview, Wayne took the stairs two at a time, hating to keep his friends waiting. But before he could reach the dressing room door, fans intercepted him. "Will you sign my program, Wayne?" Wayne obligingly signed autographs for everyone who wanted one.

When he opened the locker room door, Mike asked him, "What took you so long?"

"Some kids wanted autographs. I won't be much longer. Are we still going for pizza?"

"Yeah. Del went home to change. We'll pick him up on our way."

Wayne picked up his coat. "Good, I want to change my clothes, but I want to call my folks first."

"Go ahead, we don't mind waiting."

10:10 PM

Meanwhile Joe and Helen Estes in Anaconda, Montana, turned on the TV waiting for the sports broadcast from Salt Lake City to find out the results of the game before Wayne's call. Joe started pacing. He was anxious to talk to Wayne before he left for work at the smelter. He grabbed the phone on the first ring.

"Wayne! How did the game go?"

"Dad, I wish you could have seen it. We won and I played the best game of my life. And I got the fieldhouse record."

Wayne Estes: A Hero's Legacy

"You must have been a scoring machine." Joe whispered to Helen, "He got the fieldhouse record." Then to Wayne, "How many did you make?"

"Forty-eight points—24 in each half and now I'm one over 2,000."

"That's great, Wayne. I'll get the details from Mom tomorrow. Got to get to work and Mom wants to talk to you. See you in a couple of weeks. Love you. And congratulations on the record."

"Thanks, Dad. Love you too."

Then Helen took the phone. Needing more information, she instructed, "Tell me about the record, son."

"Mom, I scored 48 points for the fieldhouse record. And it put me over the 2,000 point total. The fans gave me a standing ovation," Wayne said.

"God love ya, Wayne. I wish I could have been there."

"The Lakers told me Saturday night they want to draft me. Now they really might. Do you know what I can do with all that money? I can buy you and Dad a house of your own and send Ronnie to college. How would you like that?"

"Wayne, that makes me want to cry. I'm so proud of you. Not very many people ever get a son like you."

Wayne paused, then inquired about his ten-year-old brother, "How's Ronnie doing?"

"Just fine. He practices as much as you do. Are you in for the night?"

"Na, some of us are going for pizza. I couldn't sleep now if I wanted to."

"Well, be careful," Helen said.

"Don't worry, Mom. We'll be careful. You take care."

She closed with her usual, "God love ya, son."

He than called his girlfriend, Paula Bandy, in Provo. "Paula, I wish you could've seen the game. I played better than I ever have before.

February 8, 1965

And I'm serious about those missionary lessons. If that's what it takes to marry you, I'll do it. I know we're meant to be together," Wayne promised.

10:20 PM

As the three men headed to Wayne's apartment, they passed a horrible-looking car wreck surrounded by police cars, ambulances and crowds of people. It took the edge off their joviality but they didn't stop to gawk.

Mike honked the horn when they got to Wayne's apartment and Del came right out. Then they headed back up the hill past the accident to get pizza. Sitting at Fredrico's Wayne talked about the game. "I just played the best game of my life. I can't believe I set both records. I've known for a couple of games that I'd get two thousand points, but I wondered if I'd ever break the fieldhouse record. I can't believe I got it. I'm glad you guys came."

"I sure picked the right game to come to. You were great," Mike said.

Wanting to turn the conversation from himself, Wayne asked, "Tell us about Westminster."

"Oh, it's okay. It's warmer in Salt Lake than Logan. Everybody knows everybody, but we don't have an All-American on our basketball team."

"I haven't made All-American yet," Wayne countered. "Having UPI and AP pick you depends on a lot of things. Harvey Kirkpatrick and John Mooney think I'm a shoo-in, but I'm nervous. If only I didn't want it so bad."

"You've reached all the other goals you set, why don't you think you'll get that one?" Del queried.

"Well, I didn't make the Olympic basketball team like everyone in Anaconda and Logan thought I would. You just never know when people who don't know you get to decide your fate."

Wayne Estes: A Hero's Legacy

Del agreed as Mike and John nodded. "What did Andreasen ask you about in the interview?"

"About the records and me playing with the Lakers." Wayne responded. "Do you guys really want to hear all this?"

"Sure, we're all ears," Mike said.

Wayne continued, "He wanted to know if I'd play guard or forward. If I make it to the pros, I'll have to work on my ball handling. How do you think I'd do as a guard?"

Del answered for all of them, "Don't kid me. You're too big to play guard, and you're too good not to play forward. You'll fit in. Don't worry so much. The way you shoot, anyone would want you."

"I'm not so sure. Lots of good shooters don't make it in the pros. Remember Utah's Billy McGill and Bill Green from Colorado State?" Wayne reminded them. "But I won't complain if I just get the chance. If I don't make good after that, it's my fault, but if I don't get a chance, I'll always wonder if I could have made it."

10:32 PM

As the four visited in the restaurant, Richard Wright, a Logan City police officer, continued working at the accident scene. After all the injured had been transported to the hospital, he concentrated on writing down details and cleaning up. When he noticed a power line on the ground crossing Fourth North, he called a power company workman to come and take care of the hot wire.

As Wright scrutinized the snowy ground in the darkness for fragments from the car wreck, he passed several times under another wire, this one six-feet-four inches off the ground, without noticing it.

When Utah Power and Light worker Stuart Hardman arrived, he immediately tested the power lines along Fourth North. When he touched the drooping wire with his rubber glove, he knew it was hot. He didn't dare cut the wire because he didn't have any place to put the live end until he could get the power shut off at the switchbox, located 25 feet off the ground and five blocks away. Before Hardman

February 8, 1965

had a chance to tell Wright about the live wire, Wright took him to the wire lying across the street.

Hardman reassured the officer, "No problem. When the wire hits the street, a relay switches and the power shuts off." Hardman then rolled up the wire.

Wright then noticed the lamp bracket hanging precariously, but still didn't see the wire it was pulling down with it. "Will it fall down?"

"It might," Hardman explained. "I'm on my way to get a tall ladder. I'll be right back." Without mentioning the drooping wire, Hardman drove the four extra blocks to get the ladder.

10:55 PM

On the way home from the pizza parlor, Wayne and his buddies drove past the wreck for the third time. Since the crowd had mostly dispersed, and the ambulances had departed, Mike suggested, "Let's go look at it."

They parked three houses west of the wreck. Rather than trudge through the snow to get to the sidewalk, they walked in the street to the mangled car. The snow had started falling again, so they analytically examined how the car had wrapped itself around the pole, and then they headed back on the sidewalk to Mike's car.

Leaving the sidewalk to get to the car, Del noticed the dangling wire as he walked beneath it. He turned around, reaching back to block his friend's passage, and automatically said, "Duck, Wayne."

But his warning wasn't soon enough. Del watched in horror as his warning and restraining hand were milliseconds too late. The wire, six-feet-four inches from the ground, brushed Wayne's forehead. As the electricity shot through Wayne's massive frame, Del, propelled by the jolt he received as he touched Wayne to warn him about the wire, flew into the street. Wayne instinctively swatted at the wire with his right hand. The jolt caused his muscles to contract around the hot wire. Smoke rose from his clinched fist. He crashed to the ground pulling the 2,300 watt wire with him.

Wayne Estes: A Hero's Legacy

Crawling back to Wayne, Del pushed Mike away just as he was reaching out to Wayne. "Don't touch him! You'll get it too," Del yelled as he shakily stood up. Ironically, in their first aid class that quarter, Del and Wayne had studied what to do if someone touched a power line. Kicking the wire out of Wayne's hand as he jumped in the air, Del collapsed at Wayne's side. But knowing Wayne was hurt far worse than himself, Del roused himself to check Wayne's pulse. Nothing. "No," screamed Del, "Wayne, no!" Del tipped Wayne's head back and started mouth-to-mouth resuscitation.

Across the street, Officer Wright saw people hurrying away from the car wreck toward something on the ground. Rushing over, he verified that an individual was in need of help, ran back to his police car, and called for an ambulance. 10:57—one hour and twenty-two minutes had elapsed since the first accident. Many people had walked under the wire, including the police officers, but only one had stood six-six.

10:58 PM

Mike Chadwick, another officer, raced over to Del's side and insisted on relieving the trauma-stricken friend. He cleared Wayne's mouth and took over administering mouth-to-mouth resuscitation. Wright frantically tried to revive Wayne, administering CPR until the ambulance arrived.

Once the two-man ambulance crew got there, they decided instantly to work right there. One EMT said later, "We couldn't stop the emergency procedures for even a second." As they took over from the officers, Wright then began guarding the hot wire, not realizing Hardman, blocks away, had already shut off the power.

Nearby residents started making phone calls as soon as they learned the victim was Wayne Estes. One called Norm Seifkin, a teammate living with Hal Hale and Pete Ennenga. It took five minutes for those three to reach the scene from Bullen Hall, a men's dormitory.

Pushing their way to the front of the crowd, they were anxious to help, only to see Wayne lying all too still on the ground. When a

February 8, 1965

woman from a nearby house brought out blankets, these teammates formed a makeshift tent to protect Wayne from the snow.

Hardman returned to the scene. Having cut the power to the dangling wire, he parked next to the light pole without looking down the street at the crowd gathered around Wayne. When he cut the wires, he freed the dangling light bracket. As it crashed to the ground in the dark snowy night, those silently surrounding Wayne flinched and jumped.

11:05 PM

Within fifteen minutes of Wayne's accident, Coach Andersen left a victory party at Harvey Kirkpatrick's home. As he drove up Fourth North, he saw at least thirty people huddled around someone on the ground and a car bent around the light pole. Andersen pulled off the road. It was not his custom to stop at accidents, but he felt he should stop at this one. Parking on the south side of the street, he crossed the dark street. He asked those standing in the back, "What happened?"

Someone, recognizing Andersen, whispered, "It's Wayne."

"He's all right, isn't he?" Andersen gasped. The man shook his head no. Elbowing his way through the crowd, Andersen saw Wayne's motionless body.

When Andersen didn't return to the car, his wife Donna walked over to check on him. She numbly stood next to him as they watched the ambulance crew work fruitlessly for another forty minutes.

The crowd parted as the ambulance crew retrieved the stretcher, lifted Wayne onto it, and then pulled a sheet over him. They still couldn't believe what had happened as Wayne was carried to the ambulance. When it left without announcement, no sirens or flashing lights, Andersen wandered to some porch steps, where he sat crying, already knowing the grim outcome.

Wayne Estes: A Hero's Legacy

12:00 MIDNIGHT

The police let Andersen sob for a few minutes before asking him, "Who do you want to call Wayne's parents?"

Awaking from the nightmare, Andersen responded, "I'll have to do that. Strangers shouldn't tell them." Dr. Wendell Budge, who lived a few houses away and had watched and worked feverishly on Wayne for the past hour, invited Andersen and his wife to make the phone call from his house.

Andersen, still in shock, called John Cheek, Wayne's high school coach in Anaconda, Montana. "I need your help. There's been a car accident with a downed power line. Wayne's dead. How do I tell his folks?"

John offered to call Wayne's Aunt Elizabeth, his mother's sister. "Her husband can call Joe at the smelter and tell him of the accident. He'll want to be home when Helen receives the news. Give me fifteen minutes and then you can call the Esteses."

Lawrence Schmieding, Joe's brother-in-law, reached Joe at the smelter, "There's been an accident. You need to go home right now."

Because Helen hadn't felt well, Joe immediately thought of her, "Oh, my God, it's Mom."

"It's not Helen. Wayne's been killed in a car wreck. Helen doesn't know yet."

Terribly shaken, Joe rushed home to comfort Helen when she received the news. He was numb with shock and grief himself, but knew his wife would take the news much harder.

Meanwhile, Elizabeth called Helen's doctor. She suggested he go to the Estes home to be on hand in case Helen had a heart attack or needed a sedative. He refused saying, "She'll have to handle this on her own." Knowing Helen would need comfort as well as support, Elizabeth went right over. When Helen answered the door and saw her sister, she screamed, "What's happened to Dad?"

February 8, 1965

"Nothing, Helen. It's Wayne. He's been in an accident. Joe will be here in a minute."

When Joe arrived, he told Helen as gently as possible, "Wayne's been killed in a car wreck." Helen collapsed on the sofa and started sobbing.

Eleven-year-old Ronnie was awake by this time and heard everything. He ran to the living room and threw his arms around his mom, "Don't cry, Mamma. Don't cry." A few minutes later, Andersen called and gave Joe the accurate details. Wayne hadn't been killed in a car accident, but by a live wire left dangling for over an hour.

1:07 AM

One of the first people Helen thought of was Judy Morstein, a good friend from Butte whom Wayne had seriously dated. "I can't tell her. You'll have to get someone to call her," she said. They decided John Cheek should do it.

When the phone rang in Judy's apartment in the early morning hours of February 9, she knew it was Wayne, calling to tell her about the game. She fainted when Cheek told her what had happened.

While Andersen made phone calls to Anaconda, the people at the accident hurried away to make phone calls of their own. Word spread so fast that half the student population and adults in Logan had heard the tragic news by morning. When they tried to check the details, they learned no more than that there had been a car wreck and that Wayne had been electrocuted.

Parents discussed whether to wake their children and share the tragedy. Girls in the dorms wandered between floors looking for people to share their grief. When they found apartments with lights on, they stiffly broke the news. Boys swore and hit mirrors hoping to make the pain go away. People who didn't know Wayne personally went back to bed but couldn't sleep. Their minds couldn't stop reviewing the game. Without the facts their imaginations couldn't figure out the freak events that had taken Wayne's life.

Wayne Estes: A Hero's Legacy

Many denied the news until they personally called the police station or the hospital to confirm the death. Still they couldn't really believe it. "He can't die." "He has to finish out the season." "What about his pro career?" As people gradually accepted Wayne's death, they cursed the wire and the darkness that had destroyed Wayne's potential. The height and hands which had brought him to the pinnacle of his college career had now ended his life in cruel irony.

CHAPTER 2
BEGINNINGS OF GREATNESS

Although Joe Estes and Helen Smith grew up only thirty miles from each other in two small towns in Montana, they didn't meet until 1942, her senior year in high school. By then Joe had been working on numerous farms for several years, being seven years older than she. Joe fell for her the first time he saw her at the roller skating rink in Virginia City; it took her a little bit longer to be convinced that he was the one for her. Since the Army hadn't drafted the 25-year-old Joe by July 1942 because of a bad eye, the young couple felt like they could marry without having to worry about the war.

However, after only one month of marriage, Joe received his draft notice with orders to report to Billings, Montana, where he would be trained as a medic. Helen went with him and stayed until she found out she was pregnant. She then moved back to Virginia City to help take care of her mother, who suffered from a creeping paralysis.

Because Helen suffered complications in the last month of pregnancy, the Army allowed Joe to come home to Virginia City May 12, 1943. On the morning of the thirteenth, Joe went to Ennis to visit his parents for an hour or so. Helen had said she felt much better just having him home. But while he was there, Helen went into labor and, with a doctor attending, delivered a six-pound, twelve-ounce boy. The infant was amazingly long (22 inches) for his average birth weight.

Returning home, Joe panicked when he saw the doctor's car. As he rushed to the bedroom, he found Helen and their newborn son resting comfortably. They named him Wayne Vernon. Vernon after

Wayne Estes: A Hero's Legacy

Joe's middle name and Wayne after Joe's good friend Wayne Osburn. Several days later Joe returned to Billings, where Helen and one-month-old Wayne joined him in June. They lived there for eight months until the Army transferred him to Texas. Unable to go with him because of Army regulations and wanting to be near her brothers Bill and Harry, Helen, her mother, and Wayne moved to Anaconda.

For the next two years Helen raised Wayne and tended her mother while Joe crossed the Atlantic Ocean from London to New York City, as a medic bringing back wounded soldiers. Joe received his discharge in 1946 from Fort Douglas, Utah, at the close of World War II. Overjoyed, he hurried home to his family. Although Wayne didn't recognize his dad at first, it didn't take long for them to develop a close companionship.

Since Helen now lived in Anaconda taking care of her mother, Joe went to the Anaconda Smelter to see about getting a job. When they hired him on the spot to work the night shift, he didn't realize he had taken a job that would last for 31 years. During those early years, he worked eight hours at the copper smelter and then went to the Country Club Golf Course for another full shift putting in new greens. After that job ended, he worked afternoons at Mr. Andersen's potato cellar sorting potatoes for a little extra money.

Financial difficulties nagged the adults of Anaconda. The copper business fluctuated too erratically for anyone to feel secure. But since everyone suffered economically, the children didn't know they were missing anything. Wayne lived with his parents and grandmother in a tiny, two-bedroom rental house with a small kitchen and living room.

Helen and Joe tried to remedy the bleakness of their financial situation with inexpensive recreation and a devotion to plain hard work. Playing basketball and baseball or going camping, hunting and fishing in the hills near Anaconda cemented their family ties. And Helen and Joe's work ethic also rubbed off on Wayne.

Wayne learned early to respect his elders. He had to sleep in his parents' bedroom because his grandmother Smith slept in the other

Beginnings of Greatness

one. Helen tended his grandma all day, but he never heard her complain about having the responsibility of her mother. In the evening, Joe took over. He kindly assisted the ailing woman and never voiced resentment at having his mother-in-law live with them.

Wayne never felt deprived at not having his own room. In the summer he would sleep in the backyard surrounded by the cottonwood trees.

By age five and still an only child, Wayne had acquired many pets for friends—baby ducks, hamsters, and rabbits. He treated them gently. But at that age he couldn't understand why Pinkie, his white rabbit, always chewed up his straw cowboy hat. "Why does he do that?" he would ask his mother. "Doesn't he like me?"

While Wayne worried about his cowboy hat, Helen worried about his bed-wetting. She eventually took him to the doctor to make sure he didn't have any physical reason for his lack of bladder control. The doctor explained, "Wayne is a very intense youngster. He plays so hard and goes at such a pace during the day, his body never has a chance to relax. In sleep his body relaxes to the point his brain doesn't read the signals his bladder sends. He'll outgrow it, so don't make an issue about it."

Following the doctor's suggestion, Helen and Joe ignored the problem. Though hating the extra laundry, Helen never let Wayne know he caused her added work. And because Wayne couldn't sleep at a friend's house until he outgrew his bed-wetting, Joe would spend extra hours with him in the backyard helping him toss a small basketball through a homemade linoleum hoop. The two of them spent hours in the backyard with the basketball. Joe encouraged Wayne to get it up any way he could. When Joe had to go to bed or to work, he instructed Wayne to practice shots from a certain distance. "When I play with you tomorrow, I'll see how many shots you can make out of twenty tries. If you really want to be a great player, you'll have to practice every day," his dad encouraged.

And Wayne did. He practiced long hours alone after other kids attempted a few shots and then moved on to something else. When

Wayne Estes: A Hero's Legacy

Wayne had perfected shots from a certain spot in the backyard, Joe moved him back until he could shoot from anywhere. Wayne continued to practice this way until his death.

Helen enrolled Wayne in a private kindergarten when he was five, preparing mother as much as son for the separation full-day school would bring. On his first day of first grade at Washington Elementary, Helen stayed and stayed. After all the other mothers had left, the teacher politely ushered Helen out. The day dragged on for Helen while she waited to retrieve Wayne. On the way home, she kept looking over at him to see if school had changed him any. "Well, how did you like your first day?" she asked.

Wayne casually answered, "Better after you left."

Bette Brogan, his second grade teacher, remembers Wayne as the fat kid in carpenter overalls. He had gained a lot of weight early in his life, to the point where his mother worried about his being ridiculed. She frequently came to his defense, but when she wasn't around, he teased back, acting like a bully at times. He rarely got into fights, since no one wanted to tangle with him.

In July 1953, a few months after Wayne turned ten, Helen had another baby. Joe, Helen and the baby stopped at the ball park on the way home from the hospital. Leaving the ball game to take a look at his baby brother, Ronnie Joseph, Wayne gave his approval before hurrying back. Once home and away from his friends, he stood in awe of the tiny bundle. Wayne started calling him Rochi (Raw Chee), and everyone else followed suit. He became a very protective big brother.

The next November, Helen's mother died. Wayne couldn't stop crying when they told him. Grandson and grandmother had developed a loving relationship as she had lain in bed and listened to his tales of school and sports. He had counted on her to advise and encourage when things weren't going well. The consolation of now having a room of his own only seemed to sadden him further. The room and his home were not the same without his Grandma Mina.

Beginnings of Greatness

At about this time Wayne began exhibiting a lot of nervous energy. He would look in their fridge fifty times a day. Often he wouldn't take anything, but he had to keep moving. Acting hungry gave him an excuse to leave his books, talk to his mom or tease the dog. Years later Helen found a picture of an overweight boy wearing the number 33 looking inside a fridge. She taped it on the door because it reminded her of Wayne.

Wayne attracted all kinds of friends. He had a good attitude even though he was teased unmercifully about his weight. And he liked sports, all kinds. He could hit a baseball across the commons, but still not get a home run because of his lack of speed. He wrestled and beat every kid around. He was banned from boxing by his mother after he threw a left to the chin of a much older boy and sent him backwards almost ten feet.

By the fifth grade, he had developed a reputation about his basketball skills. Jim Furaus, who later became one of Wayne's best friends, went to an elementary school on the opposite side of town. He said everyone talked about Wayne Estes. "This guy Estes can shoot," somebody told Jim.

"Nobody can be that good," Furaus thought.

Jim later saw him on the court. "He wasn't athletic looking, but he wasn't clumsy. He had a gift. He took shots from the top of the key with confidence and accuracy. I had to eat my words; he was as good as everyone had said."

Practicing for hours shooting at the homemade basket in the backyard and at the basket on the corner light pole by the alley for five years had paid off. Wayne's team easily won the fifth-grade championship in the Anaconda Little League. However, he learned being high-point man didn't mean much when his team lost the sixth-grade championship.

No one expected Wayne to amount to much on the basketball court after his elementary school success. He was just too big, and besides, everyone said, all the other boys needed was "a little more experience."

CHAPTER 3
OVERCOMING THE ODDS

At Anaconda Junior School, Wayne's interests were fairly evenly divided between baseball and basketball. He developed a competitive spirit and a sense of his own athletic worth, mainly because his parents were convinced he had a special talent.

Joe Estes again coached his son's summer league baseball team in 1956. As Joe drove their 1946 Ford full of kids to Deer Lodge for an important baseball game that summer, he told Wayne, "I'm not going to start you today. Donny (Hatcher) needs a chance too. But if we get in trouble, I'll put you in."

Crossing an overpass, Joe ran into a guardrail. Because he had his arm resting out the window, the car's spotlight caught it, nearly severing it. Since the car behind them contained the rest of the team, they had help instantly. Using diapers to control the bleeding, they hurried Joe to Deer Lodge. Although Helen wanted Wayne at the hospital to be with her, he chose to attend the game in case they needed him to pitch.

When Joe got out of surgery, he asked how the ball game turned out. When he learned they had lost by one run and that Wayne hadn't come in to pitch in the late innings, he blamed himself for the loss. "I would have put him in when the other team got to Donny. We could have won that game with Wayne pitching."

Joe would have six different surgeries including having part of a bone in his leg grafted in his arm, but he agonized continually over

Wayne Estes: A Hero's Legacy

losing that game needlessly to Deer Lodge because he wasn't there to assure his team's success by putting Wayne in to pitch.

Playing hard on the City Commons, Wayne had a great time. His seventh-grade team won the city championship. But he experienced heartbreak for the second time when they lost the city championship in the eighth grade in extra innings.

Wayne felt no pressure to excel academically, barely earning more A's and B's than C's in seventh and eighth grades. Still Mr. Elmer Carsone, the ninth grade counselor at Anaconda Junior, encouraged him to take algebra the next year.

"But I don't like math," Wayne responded.

"You'll need it to prepare for college."

"I'll think about it," Wayne promised. At home he talked to his dad. "Do you think I should take algebra? Mr. Carsone says I'll need it for college, but I hate math."

Joe sat Wayne down next to him on the couch, "Do you remember as a little kid you hated it when I worked two jobs?"

"Yeah, but what does that have to do with algebra?"

"Well, I quit school after the basketball season ended. That meant I had to do manual labor that didn't pay as good as the desk jobs. If I could've made more money at a desk job, I wouldn't have worked two jobs and could've spent more time with you. Besides the NBA doesn't draft high school kids. To play in college, you have to keep your grades up. Sign up for algebra," Joe insisted.

Wayne followed his dad's counsel. However, he still didn't study as much as his teachers wanted him to as a ninth grader at Anaconda Senior High School.

Wayne lived too far from any gym to practice there daily, so he continued to shoot baskets in his backyard. His dad had long since replaced the homemade linoleum hoop with a regular one. Neighbors

Overcoming the Odds

grew accustomed to the sound of ball against backboard long after dark and early in the morning.

But he didn't just shoot basketballs during his free time. When his friends took up tennis, Wayne beat everybody without ever practicing. Not only could he run forever, he also had a strong arm for back hands and serving. He won the horseshoe pitching contests besides the marble championship. Sitting in the alley, he threw water balloons at the Harlem Club 200 feet away to see how far he could throw and to work on his accuracy.

Living a mere few blocks from City Creek drew Wayne into fishing. Having gained a reputation for pulling out big ones, one day he snuck over the fence at the fish hatchery and netted a lunker. He bragged as he showed it off but couldn't resist telling everyone how he got it. The joke wasn't funny if only he knew it.

As Wayne continued to shoot and shoot and shoot, Ronnie tried to imitate him. Wayne felt sorry for his four-year-old brother, who didn't come close to making a basket. Wayne worked with him on dribbling until his dad made another linoleum hoop standing about four feet off the ground. They daily shot at their baskets and talked sports. This helped develop a close relationship between these two though there were ten years difference in their ages.

Beginning his freshman basketball season playing guard, Wayne stood five-foot-ten and weighed 250 pounds. Because the school didn't have a uniform to fit him, Katherine Cheek, the varsity coach's wife, took the biggest uniform home and inserted a gusset in each leg. It fit Wayne fine, but when Katherine tried it on, she got both of her legs in one leg of the shorts.

That 1958 freshman team[1], coached by Ben Tyvand, had "height, speed and crack shots," winning twelve straight games until Butte Central beat them. Wayne, the "crack shot," had a 46-point game and

[1] The "Fabulous Frosh" consisted of Wayne, Jack Schultz, Jim Devich, Tom Greenough, Tom White, Pat Connors, Jim Sullivan, Butch Lujan, Eugene Meyer, Mike Crum, Gene Keaton, Dexter Leonard, Ace Brown, Mickey Heaney, Pat MacLemore with Ben Tyvand as coach and Jim Furaus and Dale McNeil as managers.

Wayne Estes: A Hero's Legacy

led the team in scoring with a seventeen-point average, but didn't contribute much on defense. The "Fabulous Frosh," as they nicknamed themselves, went sixteen and one for the season.

While making a name for himself in basketball, Wayne also was working on his track skills. Many people considered track his best ticket to college. As a freshman, he made the high school track team and entered region competition. He received his first school letter from the points he won in the shot put and discus.

Wayne's high visibility because of his athletic prowess and large size didn't always serve to his advantage. During the summer following Wayne's ninth grade year, Wayne went camping with some of his friends at a public campground. During their stay a toilet was vandalized. After the police interrogated some kids, Wayne's name came up as a possibility. When the police questioned him, he denied having any knowledge of it. Stopping at the school to chat with Mr. Carsone a few days later, he complained bitterly, "There were dozens of kids there. Why did I get blamed? I didn't do it."

Mr. Carsone sat patiently as Wayne paced, ranting on. When he stopped for a moment, Carsone said, "Wayne, because of your athletic ability, you're in the public eye. You stand out in a crowd; and when people think who was there, your name comes to their minds. Envious people won't mind getting you in trouble. If you step out of line, some will gladly report you. Just make sure you're always innocent. Remember everyone expects good things from you."

Wayne would remember that advice, although he would not always heed it.

Wayne didn't play football until his sophomore year in high school. Because Helen worried about Wayne getting hurt, she wouldn't let him play Little League football or compete on the junior high team. Wanting him to concentrate on basketball, Joe supported that decision. Wayne wouldn't have minded except he missed the association with his best friends.

By his sophomore year, everyone expected someone of his size to play football. His parents let him make his own decision on whether

Overcoming the Odds

to play or not. Of course, he joined the team. Varsity Coach Chuck Williams rejoiced knowing Wayne's 235 pounds would help the offensive line tremendously. He also contributed with his quickness, speed and strength, controlling the line on defense. The season ended with four wins, four losses and one tie.

Wayne's intensity during games wasn't enough to keep Williams, who liked to have complete control of his ball players, from getting frustrated when Wayne kept things loose at practice and before games. Wanting dedication every minute, Williams got after Wayne for goofing off and not working as hard as he wanted him to. "I want to win this game," the coach yelled.

Looking him straight in the eye, Wayne growled, "You think I don't?" No matter what Wayne did, he knew the bottom line—winning.

After working out with the football team each afternoon until 5:00 or 5:30, Wayne stayed after everyone else had left and practiced kicking extra points and field goals. Following dinner, he went to the gym for an hour or so to work on basketball. Joe and Helen didn't mind that Wayne spent almost no time studying. They encouraged Wayne's love of sports.

After getting to bed late after Friday football games, Wayne got up early while his family slept in. He would leave a note on the table saying, "If anyone wants me, I'm at the gym."

Saturday nights found him attending Midnight Mass at St. Peter's Cathedral with his Catholic friends. He didn't want to change religions as he was raised Episcopalian, but he just didn't want his friends doing things without him. After coming home late from Mass, Wayne slept in Sundays. At noon he would once again go to the Daily Gym to shoot two hundred or more free throws.

When football season ended, he spent twice as much time in the gym. He would start shooting from one corner, move four or five feet after making at least three in a row from that position until he had shot

Wayne Estes: A Hero's Legacy

from everywhere on the gym floor. To wrap up his individual practice, summer or winter, he shot 90 to 100 free throws. This paid off while performing for the Anaconda Copperheads under John Cheek.

Cheek moved Wayne from guard to center for his sophomore year since he had grown from five-ten to six-two and had lost twelve pounds. Cheek had earlier nicknamed Wayne "Crisco," because of his huge size. Cheek continued to use the nickname throughout high school, even though Wayne seemed to slim down the taller he got. Wayne's first starting role came against Billings. He played so well that he started every game for the Copperheads and made Second Team All-State with 277 points for the 1959 season.

Wayne continued to goof off before games to ease the tension building inside himself. That year as the team went in private cars to Great Falls in a terrible blizzard, Wayne needled Coach Cheek all the way.

Cheek reminded Wayne, "You're not so tough, Crisco."

"I can beat you up anytime," Wayne countered.

"We'll see who can beat up who," Cheek challenged. On McDonald Pass, Cheek stopped the car and turned to Wayne. "Get out so I can whip you."

When Cheek got out, Wayne leaned over and locked the door. An astonished Cheek stood in the snowstorm, beating on the car window. Wayne laughed and made faces at Cheek, finally unlocking the door. The team inside didn't worry about Wayne getting in trouble. Cheek liked a good joke as much as Wayne.

Between seasons when Wayne and his friends didn't have Friday night games, they went to the Shamrock Garage to watch the Friday Night Fights on TV. Anything athletic interested Wayne. Hearing the commentators say that jumping rope improved footwork, he started jumping rope to improve his quickness. Whatever would help his basketball game, he did.

Overcoming the Odds

In track he improved his shot put distance to 51' 2½", the best in the state for a sophomore. But Wayne also entertained the rest of the team with his other track skills. In practice, he started catching the javelin on the fly.

He told his teammates, "There's nothing to it. If you have good eye-hand coordination, you just know when to wrap your fingers around the pole. If you think you can, I'll teach you." Bruce Blattner took him up and learned how to do it too.

But academically Wayne did not excel. His sophomore English teacher, Mrs. Ruby MacDonell, couldn't understand why Wayne didn't worry about his grades. When they read Shakespeare, he didn't pay attention; and he wouldn't read aloud in class when asked. He once explained to her, "I can't make my mouth talk like that. I can read and understand Spanish easier than Shakespeare."

When told he would only get a C for his year's grade, Wayne replied, "A C doesn't bother me. I want a basketball scholarship, not an academic one." He did admit to her that, "Shakespeare makes more sense than geometry. I don't think the best teacher in the world could make that class easy for me. And Mr. Richardson can see that. He says I'm one of those people whose brains won't grasp geometry concepts."

However, when it came time for him to register for his junior schedule, Wayne signed up for tougher classes: Advanced Algebra, Solid Geometry, English 11, Spanish II and U. S. History. He listened to teachers and counselors who told him what he needed to be prepared for college.

Wayne, like the rest of the teenagers in Anaconda, didn't have a summer job. They considered themselves lucky if their dads worked. Any odd jobs were given to college students.

Wayne showed off his strength several times that summer. Hunting with Tom White, Wayne packed out Tom's four-point, 300-pound deer, showing his superior strength. When John Cheek moved

Wayne Estes: A Hero's Legacy

into his new house on Park Street, he asked the basketball players for help. As they hauled a freezer full of meat out of the basement, Cheek put four teammates on one end and Wayne on the other.

During that summer's baseball season, Joe Estes worked his vacation around the ball game schedule so that Wayne wouldn't miss any games. Joe instilled in Wayne, "If you join a team, you give one hundred percent in every game and practice. When you participate in a team sport, you put the team first and your wants and needs second."

Earlier that spring, Wayne pitched on an American Legion baseball team. He looked forward to the season following his sophomore year. But during one of the games, Wayne hit a batter with a fast ball. Wayne realized that he had the potential to kill someone with a ball going eighty to eighty-five miles an hour.

A few days later he told the coach, "I want to play first base." When the coach waited for an explanation, Wayne said, "I won't pitch again." As an afterthought he added, "I don't want to hurt anyone."

"You better think about that," the coached warned Wayne. "If you don't pitch, I won't play you. We need a pitcher not a first baseman."

But Wayne didn't give in. Several more weeks passed before he went back to the coach. "Will you let me play first base?"

The coach cursed Wayne and told him, "I don't want 'fraidy cats' on my team!"

Wayne didn't play organized baseball again. His dad and mom felt bad about that decision, but knew they couldn't force Wayne to do something he didn't feel right about.

Instead he played fast pitch softball on the Commons with his friends not involved with Legion baseball, and he loved it. Most people expected him to play first base or catcher, but he played short stop, exhibiting his great throwing arm and good range. He could also hit home runs almost every time he came to bat.

Overcoming the Odds

Wayne's junior year started off with an interesting twist. His peers elected him Junior Class President. Sitting in the auditorium with the entire class, they looked over their classmates and called out names from the floor. It wasn't much of a contest. More than just the athletes felt that he was their friend.

Occasionally, Wayne's lack of seriousness got him into trouble. Coach Chuck Williams never did get used to Wayne's joking and clowning around. On the way to Livingston, their next-to-last football game in his junior year, someone in the back of the bus began calling in a soft, high-pitched voice, "Muzie, Muzie, Muzie," Williams's nickname.

When Williams turned around, silence met him. Williams knew exactly where the voice came from. He called Wayne and Jim Tarkleson to him. "Jim, I can't do anything about you since you're a senior, but Wayne, I don't want you to come out for football next season. You don't want to play football—you just want to have fun."

"Do you really mean that?" asked Wayne in subdued tones.

"Yeah, I do. I don't want guys who just get down to business during games; I want guys who are serious at practice and prepare mentally before the game. Go sit down and think about what I said." Knowing the coach meant what he said, Wayne began thinking of ways he could get back in Williams's good graces.

Since Cheek and Williams were friends and co-workers, Wayne went to Cheek for advice. "Don't worry. He'll get over his anger if you'll treat him with respect from now on. Show him you can take discipline from him." For the rest of the year, Wayne made sure he was on his best behavior whenever he was around Williams.

Cheek also helped Wayne achieve a balance in his personality. He gave Wayne a bad time about his weight, his grades, and the pranks he played on others. Cheek didn't single Wayne out for special treatment at practices or games—except when it came to the pregame meal of peaches, toast, and tea. At the beginning of the season, Wayne missed the pregame meal because Helen forced him to stay home to eat the steaks she cooked for him.

Wayne Estes: A Hero's Legacy

Helen explained that Wayne had to have meat in order to have enough strength and energy for the entire game. Soon Cheek had a steak for Wayne while the others still snacked on toast and peaches.

Cheek also had the school custodian give Wayne a key so he could practice any time he wanted. Cheek would sometimes come in when Wayne practiced. Cheek continually cheated and would push Wayne out of bounds to keep him from scoring. Other times shuffling his feet to create static electricity, Cheek would shock Wayne on the backside as he got ready to shoot. Wayne hated it. Cheek would promise not to shock him, knowing he would do it again if Wayne had the upper hand.

Wayne always had the support of his parents. Through junior high and high school the Esteses arrived first at all the games. Watching the kids warm up, they couldn't understand parents who showed up after the game started or who didn't bother to come at all.

Not attending one of Wayne's practices bothered Joe, but missing a game because he had to work made him sick. When he worked swing shift, he tried to trade days. When that didn't work, he took vacation time or called in sick.

After this had happened several times, Joe's supervisor called him in. "The boss is thinking of laying you off since you've missed work so often lately. I'd watch it if I were you." After that, Joe had to miss a few games here and there to keep his job, but Helen didn't miss a single junior high or high school game.

Helen, once frustrated with rude Livingston fans, hit someone with her purse. Another time, in a game where the refs had harassed Wayne as much as the opposing fans, Helen took up her complaints with the referee before the second half. As the Copperheads came back onto the floor, Wayne looked up. "Ah-oh, my mom's got the referee by the neck."

Wayne had to fend off more than opponents. Tanna Nazer, a sophomore girl in the pep club with short, dark curly hair and brown

Overcoming the Odds

eyes, ran up to him after every game giving him a big hug and kiss. As Wayne hadn't ever been on a date, he didn't know what to do, so he stood there with his hands at his side. Since he didn't know how he felt or what he should do, he talked to his dad. "I like her, but I don't love her. When did you know you loved Mom?"

"Oh, I'd seen her several times at the skating rink and knew I wanted to date her," Joe reminisced. "I found out she was going roller skating so I went hoping to get a date."

"Well, did you skate with her?" Wayne asked, suddenly interested in the budding romance of his parents.

"No, she sat on the sidelines all night; but every time I skated by, she stuck her foot out trying to trip me. I knew then she liked me too. After that night, we spent a lot of time together even though she was still in high school. I figured I was pretty lucky to go out with the most popular girl around. I don't think I would have gotten married if she had married anyone else. When you feel like that, you'll know you're in love. Until then, it's best to be good friends with all of them."

That year the Copperheads went to the State Tournament held in Great Falls. A rival coach commented to the press on Wayne's superlative play. "Estes, just a junior, will likely become the top hand in AA circles next season." Another coach added, "At 6' 4" he's not tall enough to be a collegiate center man and he moves a little too slow to be a college forward." Someone else replied, "That may be, but boy, can that 'big lad' use his weight to good advantage in high school competition." Wayne led all scorers in the "Big Ten" and was named to the State Tournament's first team.

Wayne had definite opinions about certain personal habits. When his friends tried smoking, he wouldn't go along. Giving them a bad time for trying it, he crushed any cigarettes he saw. He didn't offend his friends though; he sometimes put the cigarettes out with a dainty flick and the next time he stomped on them like Smokey the Bear.

Wayne Estes: A Hero's Legacy

It was the standard of the day for the basketball team to wear hats and overcoats to away games. Some of the team started shoplifting little items as they wandered through stores before going to the gym. Wayne questioned their actions, but didn't preach or judge. The practice stopped before anyone got caught.

However, one of Wayne's bad habits caused a lot of consternation to his parents. He consumed a lot of beer with his buddies. His parents didn't approve of his drinking, but they knew they couldn't stop him unless they never let him out of their sight. Whenever Helen suspected the boys planned on taking beer, she encouraged him to also take his sleeping bag and spend the night. Wayne knew that was her way of saying, "Don't drink and drive." Helen was way ahead of the time when that slogan would become commonplace.

Wayne's group of athlete friends confined their drinking to the summer or between sport seasons. This made it easy for them to keep training rules and concentrate on their skills. But when Wayne did drink in the off season, he would drink over a dozen beers at a time, not showing many obvious effects because of his massive size. His behavior usually consisted of silly imitations of coaches, refs, teachers, and opposing players.

Parents and coaches in rural Montana in 1960 knew about the drinking but had the attitude, "Boys will be boys." As long as it didn't get out of hand and didn't happen often, no one tried to stop them.

Part of Wayne's responsibilities as the Junior Class President was to lead the Grand March at the Junior Prom. His mom taught him how to dance and made him get a date. He asked his good friend, Budie LeBlanc, knowing she wouldn't turn him down. She couldn't have been happier about going with the most popular person in school. After he got home, he was pretty excited to tell his parents, "That wasn't near as bad as I thought."

Later that spring, Wayne competed in the shot put event in the National Junior Olympics. David Rivenes, Chairman of the Junior Olympics Committee Montana Association of the AAU (Amateur

Overcoming the Odds

Athletic Union), informed Wayne that his throw of 59 feet was the second longest in the country for his age.

During Wayne's junior year at the state track meet, Norvel "Nog" Hansen, a Utah State graduate and the head football and track coach at Helena High School, felt Wayne could contribute to a college track program, after watching him throw the shot 56' 11I" and the discus 143' 11H". He encouraged Wayne to attend Utah State and participate in track or football. He talked about Ralph Maughn and the national champions he had coached at USU in the discus. Wayne already knew of Olympian L. J. Sylvester and thought highly of him. Hansen reminded Wayne, "L. J.'s still in Logan helping with USU's discus throwers." When Wayne expressed the desire to play basketball instead, Nog recommended that Wayne keep all his options open.

Wayne's confidence in sports didn't carry over to other situations though. He put off getting his driver's license when he turned sixteen in May because he was afraid he would fail the written test. His mother repeatedly warned him about driving illegally, but he made allowances for himself. "Mom, I'm so big no one will stop me. Besides I'm a careful driver."

Wayne didn't often ask for the car, and when he did, Helen couldn't tell him no if their car was available. He proved his ability by never getting a ticket or getting in an accident. Helen didn't insist he take the test until the summer after his sophomore year in college when he started taking some of the young boys home from work at the recreation department. At that time she teased him mercilessly for putting it off so long because he passed the test on the first try.

Wayne's summer between his junior and senior years of high school was carefree and full of the types of adventures that pushed the limits of legality and sometimes bordered on sheer recklessness. In midsummer the group went to Tom Greenough's cabin near Silver Lake. Since they didn't have indoor plumbing someone had to go to the river for water. Wayne and Jack Schultz agreed to go fetch the water if the others would do the dishes. They started out with two flashlights and two buckets each. As they passed by a stump in the

Wayne Estes: A Hero's Legacy

dark woods, they heard a growl. Their flashlights caught the head of a mountain lion as it reared over the stump. Wayne took off through the timbers while Jack stood frozen in his tracks. Only later did they discover Tom had placed a mountain lion head on a box and crouched next to it with a coat over himself.

A few days later, they spotted a bear twenty feet across the swamp while they were fishing. While the boys whistled to make it turn around, the bear lumbered off, looking back over its shoulder several times. A short time later, the bear came crashing through the trees straight at them. Jim, who was on the same side of the swamp as the bear, climbed a tree. The others threw rocks trying to get the bear to move. The bear got mad and reared up after Jim. The boys, frightened for Jim, jumped on a shed with an aluminum roof until the bear left. Wayne reenacted the entire scene that night, playing the parts of Jim, the bear, and the group jumping on the roof.

Knowing that no one would think he was still in high school because of his size, Wayne began going to bars that summer to listen to rock and roll music. He rarely asked anyone to dance. When someone asked him, he made excuses. "I'm a basketball player, not a dancer." But that didn't stop him from going and enjoying himself. If only Wayne and one friend went, they stayed for quite a while; but if more went, they invariably drew attention to themselves. Managers would chase them out for being underage. They couldn't wait until they could legally enter bars.

One summer night Wayne and his group of friends went to the Dirty Bowl, a bar with a dance floor on the west side of town. As the guys visited in the rest room, Wayne sat on a washbasin. It broke off the wall. They all slipped out of the rest room quietly without saying anything. Within five minutes, the manager asked Wayne who pulled the washbasin off the wall. He admitted he broke it. He paid for a new sink and also offered to help install it so the manager wouldn't call the police on him.

Because of a fight, the police showed up one summer evening at a dance at the Daily Gym. They parked their car in front and ran up

Overcoming the Odds

the steps. Wayne and his gang left the gym via the fire escape because of the problems. But seeing the squad car with its motor running was just too big a temptation. They moved it to an alley and hurried back to the gym.

The police left the gym, only to return seconds later to begin interrogating everyone. Wayne kept a straight face as he said he saw some unknown hoods jump in and drive off. It took the police a while before they located their missing car. And if they ever really found out who took their car, they never took action against them.

One August evening, while playing softball on the Commons, Wayne met a kid from California traveling cross-country on a ten-speed. He asked Wayne, "Ever hear of mooning?"

"What's that?" Wayne wanted to know.

"You pull down your pants and show people your buns. It's the rage in California," the cyclist said.

This new gag was too much for Wayne to pass up, and he had the perfect opportunity to "moon" when his dad dropped him and some of his friends off at Squaw Rock at Rock Creek one Thursday for a weekend camping trip. That first day while his friends readied their fishing rods, Wayne left the group and hid in the bushes by the trail. As they passed by, he shoved his bared rear end out at them. His friends loved the prank but they didn't pull it in town.

That summer Tanna Nazer and Wayne became an item. They spent a lot of time together at each other's homes. Their dates consisted mostly of Tanna attending Wayne's softball games. Helen, always the protective mother, sat by Tanna at these games and let her know that although Wayne enjoyed Tanna's company, he wasn't looking for a serious relationship. Tanna agreed, but that didn't end her crush on the "best looking guy in Anaconda."

CHAPTER 4
THE GLORY YEAR

As the summer ended, Wayne's thoughts turned to football. Two weeks before school started, the coaches and managers handed out uniforms and pads. Wayne, afraid Williams wouldn't let him play, stood behind the building and had his friends sneak him all the equipment he needed. Suspecting something, Williams stalked around the building to find a humbled Wayne. "Do you really want to play?" Williams asked.

"I do, Coach. I'll work hard and try not to goof off before games or at practice," Wayne promised.

Williams had wanted the big, strong player all along, but on Williams's terms. He let Wayne know what he expected of him and told him to report to practice the next day. That year Wayne played center on offense and tackle on defense besides kicking the extra points. He begged Williams to let him try a field goal in a game, but the coach never relented. Wayne's stamina paid off since he had to be on the field almost the entire game, but to the opponents' dismay, his strength and desire didn't wain in the fourth quarter.

At that time Anaconda's enrollment had increased to 700 students, grades ten through twelve, so the ninth graders remained at the junior high for the first time in seven years. The Copperheads played in the "Big Ten" conference, which included any school within a 150-mile radius with 600 or more students. Because of the distance between schools, every team spent hours riding the bus throughout the season.

Wayne Estes: A Hero's Legacy

The distance didn't keep the parents and fans from making every effort to attend the games.

The Lettermen unanimously elected Wayne president of the A Club, a club for those who had earned a sports letter. Wayne with two letters in football, two in basketball and three in track had two more letters than any other athlete at the school. The club also recognized him as the best athlete leader at Anaconda High. Having the respect and support of the other athletes meant a great deal to Wayne.

At that time, Jim Furaus, the Key Club President, began pressuring Wayne. "Why don't you join the Key Club? You should get involved in something other than athletics."

"What would I have to do?" Wayne asked.

"Attend meetings and do service projects for the community. It looks good on a job application," Jim promoted.

"Might as well," Wayne said.

The club had inherited a debt from the former advisor since no one had ever sold the license plates he had ordered. No one wanted the job of selling the plates, but Wayne took it on after pressure from Jim. Wayne used every wily tactic he knew to coerce friends and strangers into buying the plates. Some said he twisted a few arms, quite literally. But he helped get the club out of the hole.

Busy with Key Club, classes, and dating Tanna, Wayne still put his best concentration into his football game. He had high expectations for the team his last year in high school. A loss to Butte early in the season only made him try harder. Two weeks after losing to Butte, Anaconda beat the Bengals from Helena seven to six. Since Helena had scored first, Wayne had to make the extra point for the victory. The next week when they played Great Falls, Wayne had his chance again. With Anaconda trailing six to nothing, Williams paced up and down on the sidelines. He called a timeout and ran onto the field after Anaconda made a touchdown. Wayne put his arm around Williams before he ran back to the sidelines, "Coach, I'm going to get the extra

The Glory Year

point. You don't have to worry." Wayne's kick almost hit the scoreboard another twenty yards beyond the goal posts to win the game seven to six.

Wayne's football career came to a climax when the Montana press named him the All-State Center first team in the AA Football Conference, which meant he would play for the West Shrine Team on August 26 at Helena. Coach Williams was to praise his star 25 years later, "Wayne was the finest lineman I ever coached."

Wayne had let his studies slip significantly during football season. After a particularly hard chemistry test, Wayne and his friends complained, "Too bad we can't study directly from the test questions. There must be a way to get them off the board before class." Standing on a chair in the hallway to look through the high windows that ran along the classrooms next to the ceiling was too obvious. However, Wayne noticed he could see the blackboard if he stood on his tiptoes.

During lunch the day of the next test, he read the questions off the board while his friends sat on the floor writing them down. Their plan backfired as they spent all their time writing down the questions and had no time to look up the answers. Their test scores didn't improve. On the next test, they studied together the night before instead, this time improving their scores. They knew if they wanted a good laugh, they should get the questions off the board; but if they wanted good grades, they needed to study.

Wayne was well-liked by his teachers, despite his inattentiveness to his studies. His size put him on a friend-level with many of them, and he was allowed liberties usually given only good students. His teachers followed his athletic career, even after he graduated.

Wayne didn't mind seeing the football season end so he could get down to the serious business of basketball. He had managed to visit the gym daily during football season to practice free throws and hook shots. Tanna often acted as ball boy during these solo practices, but she was easily bored and never understood his drive to continually improve his shots.

Wayne Estes: A Hero's Legacy

The Anaconda Class of 1961, with many outstanding athletes playing basketball[1], considered Wayne at six-feet-six-inches and 245 pounds the best. He could play inside, outside, rebound, pass, and score from anywhere on the court. His weakness was defense; his strength was that he was a team player. He never slighted his teammates.

As the team traveled to Coeur d'Alene, Idaho, for their first game, a team undefeated on their home court, Cheek reminded them, "Don't be too cocky. One guy is 6' 10" and two are 6' 7". Their guards are over six feet."

The team, used to Cheek's hyperboles, weren't shaken. But walking into the gym where the Coeur d'Alene team warmed up, the Copperheads realized Cheek hadn't exaggerated much. Anaconda won the tip off, but the 6' 10" center knocked Wayne's first hook out of bounds. The Copperheads soon regrouped to overpower them and eventually defeated them for the hard-fought victory.

The boys in the senior class that year were close knit, athletes and nonathletes alike. The football players who didn't participate in basketball and others who couldn't stand missing any of the action, attended every basketball game. They acted like a pep club: cheering and supporting their friends.

The varsity basketball team were good friends on and off the court. After home games, the team received a ticket for a free milk shake at Thompson's Drive-in. Cheek also handed each a silver dollar for hamburgers and fries. Most often they pooled their money to buy chicken or spaghetti.

After many games, they stayed up most of the night waiting around until the *Anaconda Standard* came out so they could read about the victory and find out how the other teams had fared. Hating to break up the fun, they sometimes went ice fishing instead of going

---

[1] The starters consisted of 6' 3" Tom Greenough and 6' 2" Ace Brown at forwards, 5' 10" Jack Schultz and 6' 0" Pat Connors at guard with Wayne at center. The other team members were Jim Devich, Mickey Gee, Tom White, Mike Crum, Steve Clark, Jack Nielson, and Sam Ulstad.

The Glory Year

home to sleep all morning. Often, Wayne would stop to pick up his seven-year-old brother who would join them for an hour or two.

Wayne had eleven 30-point games his senior year besides leading in rebounds. Wayne's rebounding ability allowed his teammates to shoot from outside. If they missed, Wayne put the rebound in.

Wayne saw the dark side of sports too. He received all kinds of abuse on the court, probably more than any other high school student that year. Boos and crude remarks became a regular occurrence at visiting schools. When the Copperheads walked out of the visitor's dressing room to warm up, they saw signs all over the gym such as "Estes is a porker."

At Billings, people spit on him. He received standing ovations whenever the ref called an infraction on him because opponents wanted him to foul out. When Anaconda played Livingston, fans called him a "fat s.o.b."

Many high school athletes would have become mean or gotten in fights faced with this type of abuse. Jim Wedin, a high school basketball official who worked many of Wayne's games, said, "He had to take a lot of abuse, but he didn't let the harassment affect the way he played."

One school did begrudgingly give Wayne some respect. A keen rivalry existed between Anaconda and Butte, but by the time Wayne reached his senior year, Butte realized Wayne was something special. They clapped when he got a foul, but they didn't ridicule him like the other schools did. In the middle of the game with Butte, the announcer broke in with, "A vehicle from Anaconda is blocking traffic. Would someone please move 'Car 54'?" Both sides of the stands roared as Wayne in jersey number 54 acknowledged the joke.

Helen and Joe, worried about Wayne's increasing involvement with Tanna, put pressure on Wayne to stop dating her. They felt he had too much ahead of him to think about getting married. He respected his parents' logic and decided he should date others. But he had a difficult time talking to Tanna about it. His friends tried to help by arranging a couple of dates with perky Marlene Bucholz.

Wayne Estes: A Hero's Legacy

One February night Wayne met Marlene downtown at Bill's Drive-in. As they talked, Tanna came in and saw them together. Shocked and angry, she still couldn't get him to talk about their relationship.

The next Friday night he had already set up a date with Tanna to go to the Youth Center dance. The entire night he remained silent. He couldn't think of anything to say. When Tanna tried to talk to him, he ignored her. After a while, he asked someone else to dance. Frustrated and jealous, she took him aside after that dance almost yelling, "I want to talk to you." That got everyone's attention. When he bent down to listen, she slugged him as hard as she could. It didn't leave a mark, but it did embarrass him. Everyone started to snicker. Before she walked away, she kicked him so hard she broke her little toe. She limped off the floor and left the center. They never dated again. Wayne later said he regretted the immature way he had handled the whole situation, but then it had been his first experience with breaking up.

Wayne's bad luck with love didn't stop him from interfering in other's love lives. He set up his good friend Jim with a short-haired brunette named Mary Lou Clark. He hit the mark with this match. Jim and Mary Lou married two years later.

Wayne and the Copperheads won their four preseason games and all eighteen in league play, setting a record as the first team in the history of the AA Conference in Montana to complete a season undefeated. They also set the Memorial Gym record at Anaconda High for most points scored in a game when they defeated Kalispell, 91–64. This was also the most points in a single game ever scored by any Anaconda team. Always wanting to win, Wayne gave a hundred percent during this streak.

The Copperheads counted on Wayne to maintain his scoring pace and get his share of rebounds to keep the offense rolling in the state playoffs that started March ninth. They won their twenty-third straight victory of the year beating Great Falls by ten. Wayne paced the team with twenty points.

The Glory Year

Wayne's 23 points weren't enough for Anaconda to beat Livingston in the second round, a team they had beaten twice during the regular season. Wayne and his teammates wept openly after the game they lost 70–51.

Coach Cheek wondered if they could come back the next morning and play Butte Central after losing their chance for first place the night before. Wayne rallied everyone. "We're still the best team in the state, but no one will believe that if we don't come back today and win. Forget last night and concentrate on today. After what we've done this year, we don't want to go home before the final night."

Anaconda fought down to the wire, finally pulling out a 57–55 victory in overtime. Wayne had high-point honors with 33. In their final game with Billings, Wayne scored 31 points and they took third place. They ended their season with the best over-all record in the state—25 wins and only one loss.

Wayne had tallied 1,432 points in his three years—277 as a sophomore, 534 as a junior, and 621 as a senior. His 430 points in Class AA conference play for eighteen games during the regular season broke the record of 428. His scoring average of 23.8 points per game set a new record for any Anaconda High School player.

He led Montana's "Big Ten" high school circuit during both his junior and senior year. Coaches and sports writers named Wayne to the State Tournament's first team for the second year in a row.

Two weeks after the state tournament, Wayne started track for his final year, again specializing in the shot put and discus. After a week of work-outs, Coach Williams wanted to record their throws to rank them in their events. Borrowing the junior high's eight-pound shot, Wayne sneaked it into the stadium before practice. After Williams had measured two or three throws for each person, Wayne entered the pit and threw that little shot as hard as he could. It went right over Williams's head and hit the rock wall at the end of the stadium. The throw impressed Williams for a split second before he realized what Wayne had done. Williams chased Wayne across the football field and

Wayne Estes: A Hero's Legacy

out the stadium gates. Wayne didn't come back to practice that afternoon; but when Williams drove by the stadium that evening, he saw Wayne practicing his throws.

During the regular season, Wayne threw the shot 59' 4¾", almost three feet more than the official interscholastic record of 56' 6" early in the season. A week later at a Four-city meet, he threw the discus 160' 10" and the javelin 160 feet before the state track meet.

At his final state track meet, Wayne scratched twice in the discus trials. He had injured his wrist the day before. His dad instructed, "Reverse and qualify."

When Wayne told Williams he intended to reverse, Williams disagreed, "Do it the regular way." Wayne looked at his dad, shrugging his shoulders. He wanted to follow his dad's suggestion, but he didn't want to disobey the coach. But Joe pointed his finger at Wayne, indicating he better follow his dad's advice. Wayne reversed his throw and qualified. He ended up taking first place with a throw of 155' 7¼".

Despite his hurt wrist, Wayne also took first in the shot with his throw of 56' 4½". However, he went home extremely disappointed, not having set the state record. After the meet ended, he went back to the shot pit and threw it three times, every throw going further than the record.

Apologizing to Williams, Wayne admitted, "I don't know why I never do well in the state track meet. I guess I put so much pressure on myself to do good that I'm too uptight to do my best." He earned his fourth track letter, bringing his total of letters to ten, with three each in football and basketball.

That spring, Wayne expected to hear from some universities. Several colleges and universities had written him letters, but they didn't offer him a scholarship.

The Montana schools hadn't offered him anything. Everyone expected Montana State University in Missoula to recruit him heavily. The press had quoted Wayne saying the U was his first choice. But

The Glory Year

their new coach, Ron Nord, hadn't seen much of Wayne; and because the school had to cut the number of scholarships they could offer, he didn't want anything to do with Wayne. Nord gave no scholarships to incoming freshmen and that included Wayne.

They did offer to get Wayne jobs so that he would make enough to pay for his schooling and board and room. His dad didn't think too highly of that idea mainly because he knew Wayne wouldn't spend as much time as he needed on basketball or studies if he had to work two jobs.

Although Montana State College had seen Wayne play and knew he could shoot from anywhere, they considered him too heavy and too slow to play college ball. The MSC coach complained, "I guess they expect us to take the fat bugger." Because he didn't think Wayne, with all that weight, could make it as a college basketball player of any magnitude, he only offered him tuition, books, and fees. A couple of small schools offered him a scholarship only if he made the team and did well.

Nog Hansen, now an assistant coach at Utah State suggested to USU that they invite Wayne to spend a weekend in Logan. When the offer came, Wayne's spirits brightened although he had a research paper for John Doonhan's English class hanging over his head. Recognizing his predicament, he asked a good friend, Claudia Monoco, for help. He gave Claudia his notes and left for Logan.

When Wayne arrived at the Cache Junction Railroad Station, he relaxed when he saw Hansen's familiar face. Coach LaDell Andersen surprised him by asking many questions about his family and Montana. He could tell Andersen was interested in him as a person and not just an athlete. They talked basketball philosophy and strategy. He loved the closeness of the mountains and the warm weather, but meeting varsity ball players Cornell Green and Darnell Haney impressed him more. Eating out in fancy restaurants added to his total feeling of acceptance. Hansen told him, "LaDell and I will come to Anaconda sometime in June so we can meet your parents to

Wayne Estes: A Hero's Legacy

give them all the details. You'll want them to help you make your decision."

On the train ride home, he started worrying about his research paper. He called Claudia when he got home. She gave him good news—she had organized his notes and typed his paper. It was ready to hand in. Claudia did Wayne a real disservice when he later took Freshman English in college. He didn't know how to do a research paper.

Two weeks after the track season ended, so did school. Those who had definite plans couldn't wait for the future. Others, like Wayne, whose plans hadn't materialized, wanted the structure of school. The free time would just remind him he didn't have a future as a college basketball player.

The last week of school started with Baccalaureate Sunday night May 21 in the high school. The Reverend Robert J. McCarthy, assistant pastor of St. Paul's Church, gave the invocation and benediction. In closing, he prayed that the graduates would "So live your lives that in the hour of your death, all others will be weeping, and you will be the only one without a tear to shed. Then you shall calmly face death whenever, wherever it comes."

After the services ended, Wayne bumped and jostled his way to the front as the others left the gym. He had to talk to Reverend McCarthy. "I like the idea of living well in order to die well. I'll try to live like that from now on."

Following graduation, Wayne felt his youth and childhood slipping away. During June Wayne and Ronnie went to the Commons almost daily to play catch. Ron would squat in the catcher's position while Wayne threw to him. Ronnie had bugged Wayne for months to show him how to throw a curve, but Wayne kept telling him, "No, Ronnie. You're only seven, and that's too young for you to be throwing a curve. You'll ruin your arm."

The Glory Year

"But I won't throw it. I just want to know how. And I'm almost eight."

"Ronnie, if you know how, you'll be tempted to use it before your arm is strong enough."

Ronnie pleaded and begged and finally Wayne gave in. Ronnie promised not to use it until Wayne gave him permission. Whenever Wayne called home or talked to Ronnie, he reminded him, "Now, remember you're not to throw a curve yet. If you do, you might never pitch again. Do you understand?" He tried to pass on as much knowledge as he could to Ronnie, knowing Ronnie had the chance to do even better than he ever had.

With high school over and college three months away, Wayne had one concern—where to play basketball. The first part of June, LaDell Andersen and his assistants, recruiting in Montana, made sure they visited Wayne. After watching him play for the South squad in the North-South All-Star game in Butte on June 10, they knew they wanted him. They made the fifty-mile trip to Anaconda to visit Wayne and his parents.

Helen and Joe made the coaches feel at home. Helen and Joe asked a lot of questions but were excited for Wayne to go to Utah State when USU offered him a full-ride scholarship including tuition, books, board and room, plus a part-time job in the athletic department.

When Andersen saw Wayne's grade point, Helen explained, "You can see he spent more time in the gym than in the library."

Andersen impressed Mrs. Estes with, "He can have two tutors to help him keep up his grades. We want our athletes to get a good education and graduate. We don't want him at Utah State just to play basketball. And if he wants to participate in track in the spring, he can do that too." Andersen didn't pressure Wayne to make a decision then. "Call us when you've decided."

Before Wayne made his final decision, the Helms Foundation selected him to the Hall of Fame because of his selection to the All-State football and basketball teams two years in a row plus his records in the shot put and discus.

Wayne Estes: A Hero's Legacy

Looking at Wayne's options, Helen, Joe, and Wayne decided Utah State would be the only place for him. Helen talked to him about making good use of the tutors there. He disgustedly told her, "The day I need a tutor in college will be a cold day you know where."

"Wayne, college is harder than high school. Don't jeopardize your eligibility because of your pride," Helen warned.

"You wait. I'll show you I don't need any tutors," Wayne contradicted.

On June 29, Wayne formally accepted a Utah State athletic scholarship and left the following Monday to take a summer construction job in Logan working with brick layers. He made sure he could come home for a brief vacation the last of August to play in the Shrine football game and see Ronnie and his folks one more time before college.

On a hot July evening, Wayne and three friends went to Butte hoping to find some excitement. Although Wayne had committed to live well after graduation, that didn't mean he couldn't have fun with his friends. When they couldn't find any girls to flirt with, they drove through the known prostitution district. Wanting to see inside a house of ill repute, Wayne knocked on a door while his friends crouched behind him. The bouncer, peeping through the hole in the door, saw a six-foot-six person standing outside. Without a second thought, he opened the door. Tom White and Jim and Pat Connors ran in. When the bodyguards gathered them up, everyone gave false names and Tom's address. The bouncers told them to never come back as they kicked them out the door.

CHAPTER 5
THE NEW RECRUIT

Wayne arrived at Utah State weighing 260 pounds, looking like anything but a budding basketball star. Since he couldn't move into campus housing until school started, he moved into the Pi Kappa Alpha house, kitty-corner from the fieldhouse. That made it easy for his daily practice after work. Nog Hansen had found Wayne a hod-carrying job, carrying mortar for brick layers, but the union went on strike before Wayne had even started. Worried that Wayne might return home because of homesickness and no job, Nog scurried around until he found Wayne a road construction job. Wayne convinced Tom White, his best friend from high school, to join him in Logan for the summer when Hansen said he could also get him a job working with Wayne.

Andersen kept his eye on Wayne, making sure he had enough money to get by. Once he gave Wayne and Tom tickets for a free day at Lagoon, an amusement park in northern Utah. Not having had anything more than a carnival come to Butte once a summer, Wayne decided he wasn't missing anything if he never went there again.

At the end of August, Wayne and Tom drove home so Wayne could participate in the drills for the Shrine All-Star football game for the outstanding Montana high school football players. Wayne played offensive center and occasionally came in on defense to beef up the line. The day after the game, Wayne returned to Logan minus Tom.

Practicing alone in the fieldhouse one day, he observed Alan Parrish, the six-foot-eight All-State center from Logan High, watching

Wayne Estes: A Hero's Legacy

him. A cold feeling passed between them for a second as each recognized the other, knowing the coaches had recruited both to play center. But as they talked, the tension lessened. They began practicing together daily, each forcing the other to work harder and improve.

As the other basketball players on scholarship began arriving in Logan, they headed to the fieldhouse to start their informal practice. When they first saw Wayne, his flaws stood out. With his immense size, apparent lack of speed as he ran up and down the court, and lack of jumping ability, he looked more like a football player than a basketball talent. The team quickly nicknamed him Baby Huey, after a diapered comic strip character—he seemed like one big, happy kid.

When Darnell Haney, a varsity star and one of several blacks on the team, heard about the new recruit from Montana, he thought Wayne, coming from such a small western town, might have some trouble with minorities. Occasionally Darnell would throw a few elbows in practice because of his intensity. Wayne took it in stride and seemed to lack the prejudices his teammates kept expecting him to have. He was oblivious to color, but definitely not to talent.

During one of the first pick-up games, Del Lyons, another freshman, was assigned to Wayne's team. Del hated getting stuck with a "fatso." But he changed his mind within the first three minutes when he realized if he got the ball to Wayne, they'd keep the ball all night.

When Mick Gee, a friend and teammate from high school, came to see Wayne before school started, he sat in the fieldhouse watching Wayne work out with the team. Afterward Mick quizzed him, "Did you see Cornell Green stuff the ball from behind his back?"

"Yeah," Wayne worried. "Those guys are so good I don't know if I'll make the team. I don't think I'm good enough."

Mick disagreed. "Wayne, I didn't appreciate how good you are. I've just watched you play against Green and Haney. They're seniors and you're just a freshman. You'll not only make the freshman team; you'll start. Besides, you always worry you won't make it when you

The New Recruit

move to the next higher level. You're too dang competitive not to make it."

Wayne's teammates began to appreciate his unique skills after a few workouts. Slow of foot and handicapped because of his weight, he used his quick mind and a keen basketball sense to adapt and adjust. Much like Larry Bird, he didn't jump exceptionally well; but he had the mental gift of anticipation. With his quick hands, he got his hand on the ball if a guy beat him to the basket. Already having good scoring ability, he worked hard at positioning so he could improve his rebounding. Wayne worried he wouldn't keep up at the college level so he was always the first one to the fieldhouse and the last one to leave.

When he earned the team's respect and they found out he didn't like the name "Baby Huey," they shortened it to "Huey."

Before school started, Wayne spent a lot of time at Coach Evan Sorensen's home. A junk food addict, Wayne consumed vast amounts of anything edible. His huge appetite surprised the Sorensens. Lois, Sorensen's wife, cooked breakfast for Wayne, who ate enough for two. Then Sorensen saw Wayne eating another meal an hour later. Sorensen advised, "If you want to make the varsity team, you'll have to get your weight down."

One day, wanting to help Wayne avoid as much frustration as possible at registration, Sorensen suggested, "Let me help you figure out your first quarter schedule. It will make it easier when you go to the fieldhouse to register. First, you have to take Basic Communications."

"What's that? Don't they think I know how to talk?" Wayne couldn't keep the sarcasm from his voice.

"No, Wayne, that's a fancy name for English. And it's required of all freshmen."

"Ah-oh, that class will give me the most problems," Wayne admitted. "I fall asleep reading. I haven't ever finished a book. Mrs. MacDonell told me that would kill me in college."

Wayne Estes: A Hero's Legacy

"Why don't you take Introduction to P. E. and Fundamentals of Sports. They require thinking but not much reading. How about a psychology class?" Sorensen suggested.

"I had psychology my senior year, but I got a D out of it. Do you think I can handle it?" Wayne asked.

"Not many people have had that in high school, so you'll know more than most who take the class. Besides it fills a requirement. We want to keep you on track for graduation," Sorensen said.

"Are any other basketball players taking it?"

"Yeah, Del Lyons and probably Alan Parrish and Dave Olsen."

Wayne agreed, "Ok, I'll try it."

"You'll need another three-hour class. Anything you're interested in?" Sorensen probed.

"Na. What's an easy class where I won't have much reading or studying that will fill a group?"

"How about Art Appreciation?" Sorensen suggested. "That will give you fourteen credits, which isn't too bad your first quarter."

"Yeah, that sounds pretty easy, but could I take that Sports Officiating for Men too? I already know what jocks look for in a ref or umpire. Besides I've officiated tons of Little League games," Wayne told him.

Afterwards, Wayne wrote Mick Gee: "I sure had a wicked time registering for my sixteen credits, and I'm glad that's over. There are 2500 freshmen registered and we were all in the fieldhouse registering at the same time. What a mess!"

In the same letter to Mick, he described his social life.

I haven't been doing too much although there is a lot to do. There is something going on almost every night, although we stay home and watch movies. My roommate from California brought some stag movies. They are dirty.

The Copperheads are having a little tuff luck, Pud? Poor Muzz!! I sure hope they do good. They sure have a wicked team down here with Merlin Olsen. Their line averages 225 lbs. They

The New Recruit

are ranked really high this year. They have won all their games so far. They beat Missoula 54 to 6. They mangled them.

After classes his first day, he announced to Coach Sorensen, "I can handle English. I only have to write four themes, give three speeches, do a little reading and some grammar exercises. That doesn't sound too bad. I can always think of things to write about, and I give good speeches. The reading won't take long 'cause it's short. I'll do okay."

Wayne moved into Richards Hall when school started and continued to hang around with the football team. He had gotten to know them since they had been on campus since August preparing for the up-coming football season. Practicing daily, Wayne would finish his basketball workout about the same time the football team ended their practice, then he'd walk to the Union Building (UB) with them for dinner. Because of their friendships, the football players teased him about not playing football. He let them know he was content to help out by running the chains (marking where first downs began and ended) on the opposing sidelines and throw the football up and down the field with Alan Parrish during half time.

Wayne told of his first few weeks in a letter to his grandfather:

Well, I've been in college now for only two weeks, and it seems like two years. It isn't really too bad, but they are pouring the work on. I sure like it down here. I think I made a wise choice in coming to Utah State. I hope so!

I've decided to major in Physical Education and go into coaching. I think that is the one thing I would really like to do. My courses are kind of rough, but I think I will be able to make out.

We should have a really good freshmen team down here. They recruited some good players. They have brought kids in from California, Indiana and all over. We are going to have a tall team too. There are eight of us over 6' 4", one 6' 8" and two 6' 7". It is really going to be hard making the first team. I

Wayne Estes: A Hero's Legacy

should know in about three weeks, so I'll write and let you know.

I wish I could go hunting but I guess I won't get to come home until Christmas. I can't come home for Thanksgiving since we have a game two days after. I guess I will have to wait until Christmas.

Writing home didn't help Wayne's homesickness go away. He almost dropped out of school on several occasions that first quarter until he adopted Coach LaDell Andersen as a second father. When his new friends and activities didn't fill his needs, he went to Andersen's house to participate in some family life. Talking over his problems, eating home cooking, and playing with Andersen's five young boys helped. When he told Andersen he missed hunting and fishing, Andersen suggested Wayne talk to Del Lyons.

Walking home from the UB cafeteria, Wayne told Del how he felt. Del extended an invitation, "Get a license and go with me next weekend. We'll just go up Logan Canyon."

"Sounds great. I hope I don't make you look bad. At home they call me the Great White Hunter."

"We'll see," a doubting Del added.

When deer hunting season opened the third weekend in October, Del and Wayne took their guns up Logan Canyon. Wayne couldn't believe the warm, dry weather, unlike many hunts he'd been on in Montana. True to his word, Wayne dropped the first deer they spotted, a good-sized two-point. Pulling out his hunting knife, he rushed over to the deer and straddled it. Without any warning, the deer leaped to its feet and tried to throw Wayne off. After he wrestled the deer to the ground and cut its throat, Wayne noticed he was cut and bruised all over. Not embarrassed a bit upon returning to campus, Wayne loved showing off his battle scars and reenacting the incident.

He did complain because he broke his watch crystal in the foray. He sent the watch home to get the crystal replaced. When Helen went to pick it up, the jeweler's eyes widened, "Do you know what I found

The New Recruit

in that watch? Blood! Did Wayne get in a car accident?" Helen then spread the story to the Anaconda community.

The freshman basketball team[1], called the Ramblers, began working out every day starting the middle of October. Evan Sorensen, a demanding coach, expected more of the stars than the subs. If they didn't put out, he pulled them. He tried to teach the freshman team, nothing more than high school All-Stars, that winning meant learning how to work together. Many had never learned unselfishness or how to work hard on defense.

Alan Parrish, a Logan native, frequently took Wayne home with him. And when Wayne couldn't go home for Thanksgiving because of practices and games, the Parrish family invited him to their family celebration. The Parrishes, big people who enjoyed eating, made him feel comfortable, but he worried they wouldn't have any leftovers after he finished. Wayne was a big hit with the entire Parrish family. Before the quarter ended, Scott Parrish, Alan's eight-year-old brother who idolized his big brother, visited the team's dressing room. When Wayne broke his shoelace, he handed Scott the broken end. Scott had it hanging on his bedroom bulletin board for years after that.

Wayne loved playing in several freshmen games before Christmas but eagerly awaited the vacation. He missed his family. While at home, he received his first-quarter grades: three A's, two B's and a C in Art Appreciation (a 3.1). He reminded his mom, "And I did it without the help of any tutors."

Wayne missed his mother's cooking almost as much as he missed her. She cooked continually that vacation to make up for all the meals she thought he'd missed. And Wayne, eating like a horse, gained 23 pounds.

---

[1] The USU Freshman team consisted of Larry Angle, Gerry Christensen, Dee Hall, Ralph Hanson, Delano Lyons, Jim Mandle, Ray Minkler, George Moffitt, Mike Murry, Dave Olsen, Alan Parrish, John Rambo, Gary Schiffman, Jay Sparrow, Joe Warfel, and Wayne.

Wayne Estes: A Hero's Legacy

As soon as Wayne returned to Logan, he headed for Coach Andersen's. Andersen climbed all over him because of his weight gain. "You'll never make the varsity squad if you don't get your weight down. You better work as hard on that as you do on the other parts of the game." Then he added, "A 3.1 isn't too bad for a kid who got C's and D's in high school."

With one quarter's experience, picking classes for winter quarter didn't worry Wayne. Knowing basketball would take much more time, Sorensen suggested he take ten credits. They decided on Fundamentals of Sports, Freshman Basketball, Basic Communications and Principles of Biology.

Day after day, he practiced his famous hook shot and fifteen-foot jumper from the right baseline. This impressed members of the varsity squad. Cornell Green, Utah State's senior All-American, described Wayne as "The giant with a golden touch who had fun. He took needling real well, and he liked to clown. Everyone liked him."

Darnell Haney agreed. "The varsity teased the freshman ball players a lot, but Wayne was in a good mood no matter what we said or did to him. He was a responsive, warm human."

Wayne did get back at Cornell for all the teasing. In the middle of the season, Cornell came to practice with his head shaved. Because Wayne thought "it looked cool," he talked John Rambo and Dave Olsen into joining him for shaves too. When they showed up to the freshman game, they got stares and giggles from everyone. When the announcer introduced Cornell for the varsity game, Cornell admitted, "I was embarrassed to have my head shaved. It looked like they had started it, and that I had followed the freshmen."

Cornell, another scoring machine, appreciated Wayne's variety of shots, everything from a set, two-handed jumper, and a right- and left-handed hook. "Wayne could move outside and shoot the nets off those baskets." Two years later Cornell predicted, "Someone will draft him number one for sure."

Wayne and Mike Casey, a Snow College transfer, also related well. While Wayne kept the freshman team relaxed and loose, "Caser,"

The New Recruit

Wayne's name for Mike, did the same for the varsity. Their friendship developed to where they said they became more like brothers than teammates, having serious conversations, something Wayne didn't have with many people.

January flew by. The Ramblers, relying on Wayne, won four of their first five games. He didn't have any difficulty making the starting five like he had feared.

Leading the team to a nine and four season record, Wayne finished the year with the highest scoring average, 19.5 of any Rambler in the school's history.

After a hectic winter quarter, Wayne looked forward to going home for a few days. As soon as he walked in the door, his parents asked about his grades. Wayne gladly told them, "I haven't got them yet."

Joe asked, "Will they mail them here like they did before?"

"I don't think so. They'll put them in my registration packet."

"Well, you'll need to call or write and let us know," his mom insisted. "We want you to do well in your classes."

"How do you think you did?" his dad quizzed.

"I didn't do very well on my research paper. I didn't really know how to do it so I kept putting it off. I should have done a little bit every day. But I'll do better on the next one."

"I sure hope so. We want you to get an education. You have no guarantee you'll play basketball for a living. What classes did you sign up for this quarter?" Joe probed.

"I'm taking hard classes—American History, American Literature, and English. I can get a B in English this quarter."

"That would be nice."

"I know I have to keep my grades up to stay eligible. I'm not a dummy just because I got bad grades in high school. But don't expect all B's; nobody studies much spring quarter."

Wayne Estes: A Hero's Legacy

When he did get his second quarter grades, he received three C's and only one A. His parents didn't give him a bad time, but he knew they wanted him to do better.

Wanting to put all his time into basketball, Wayne decided not to go out for track at the conclusion of basketball season. During the spring, he shot thousands of free throws. He shot as long as he could find someone who would throw the ball back, taking the same amount of time with the other shots he developed. He worked constantly on his hook, his turn-around hook and his short jumper.

Wayne had been ambivalent about joining a fraternity. Feeling an obligation to the Pi Kaps, he and Alan Parrish had pledged with them in the fall, but had not gone active. In winter quarter, the basketball team was not allowed to go through initiation. By spring, they were under pressure to go active. The actives couldn't wait for them to go through goat week, a week of hazing for the pledges. Wayne had doubts.

The pledges didn't push him but stressed, "It'll get better once you go active." Deciding late to participate in goat week, he didn't take part in the goat show.

Following that activity, the goat master, an active responsible for all the goats, the fraternity president, and ten actives invited Wayne and Alan to an empty room. The actives decided to teach them subordination and humility. The goat master questioned Alan, "Who do you owe your allegiance to, me or the fraternity president?"

Every pledge knew the goat master was his superior until he went active. Thinking the situation over carefully, Alan replied, "The goat master."

The president stepped forward smiling. "Wrong, Alan. You owe me your allegiance." Handing Wayne a heavy wooden paddle, he added, "For not knowing the right answer, Wayne will spank you twenty times."

The New Recruit

Alan bent over as Wayne hit his backside. According to Alan, "He didn't hit me hard at first, but the actives insisted he hit harder. I was sore before the twenty times were up."

Then the goat master asked Wayne, "Who is your superior?"

Wayne had seen that the right answer wasn't "the goat master." He replied, "The president."

The goat master shook his head. "Wrong, Wayne. Now Alan will spank you." And Alan did. After a half hour, the goat master said they could leave the room. Wayne not only walked out of the room but also out of the fraternity house.

The next morning he showed up at Coach Andersen's office and talked about the night before. "I hate the hypocrisy of the whole thing. It wasn't the pain. But beating my buddy for someone's sick fun doesn't make any sense. I won't go back there again. I don't need all that demeaning crap. From now on, my teammates will be my fraternity."

Not long after that, Wayne went to the Cactus Club with a group of his friends and had too many beers. Thinking about the problems he'd had with a certain girl, he decided to settle them. He banged on her dorm door. When she didn't answer, he started throwing garbage cans. After chipping the paint on the door, spilling garbage, and denting the cans, his friends talked him into leaving. The next day he went straight to Andersen. He felt bad about the incident. When he and Andersen went back to the apartment to check on the damage, Andersen couldn't tell that anything had happened. Wayne got off without any punishment from the coach or official probation from the university.

A week or so later, he asked Mike Casey, "Are we still friends even though I acted like a jerk?"

Casey reassured him that he was still his friend but added a warning. "Learn to control yourself and your actions so they don't hurt your athletic standing."

Near the end of the quarter, Wayne and Alan Parrish began talking of their plans for the next year. Alan told Wayne that he was not

Wayne Estes: A Hero's Legacy

coming back to school in the fall, that he was going on a two-year mission for The Church of Jesus Christ of Latter-day Saints. Wayne was dumbfounded. His first question was, "How much will they pay you?"

Alan replied, "I pay my own way to go."

Wayne couldn't believe Alan would interrupt his college basketball career and give up his basketball scholarship because of his religion. He complimented Alan on his commitment, while saying, "I sure wouldn't go."

With the first year of college behind him, Wayne packed his belongings and headed for Anaconda. That summer he worked for the Anaconda Recreation Department. High school graduates ran the Little League baseball program. They dragged the infields on various diamonds to keep them as smooth as possible, set up the bases, umpired and kept score besides trying to keep peace between the parents. The elementary and junior high kids followed Wayne everywhere. Before and after their games, they walked him to the drinking fountain, sat with him while he kept score, and offered to help him rake the field between games. He knew everyone's name and showed an interest in them. Helen would ask, "Wayne, don't you ever get tired of those kids always hanging around?"

And he responded, "Mom, I just love it."

He took special interest in one child, Bobby Devine, a seven-year-old, who was partially deaf and lacked coordination. Wayne would carry him on his shoulders. Working with him hour on hour, Wayne taught him to play basketball and baseball. According to Bobby's mom, Wayne did more for Bobby than all the therapy he had ever had.

Because Elmer Carsone's son wouldn't drink milk, Mr. Carsone talked to Wayne about helping convince Vince milk would be good for him. The next time Mr. Carsone and Vince saw Wayne on the Commons, Carsone asked, "Wayne, how did you get so big?"

"Drinking milk."

The New Recruit

Vince's eyes got big before he thought of a way out. "Chocolate milk?"

Several weeks after coming home, Helen met Wayne at the door when he came home for lunch. "Your grades came this morning."

Panicked, Wayne asked, "You didn't open them, did you?"

"Why? Do you think you got an F or something?"

"Maybe in American Lit. I couldn't keep up with the reading. And when I did read, I still couldn't pick out all that symbolism crap," Wayne admitted.

"Why didn't you use the tutor?"

"Mom, tutors don't read for students, and that's what I needed someone to do."

"Well, open them. I didn't."

Tearing open the envelope, Wayne blew a sigh of relief, "I got a D! Mom, I passed. I got a D! And I got a B in English. I told you I'd do better in that class."

"Is that all?"

"No, I also got two C's. But that's okay."

A few weeks later, while Wayne was keeping score at one of Ronnie's games and Jim was umpiring, Ronnie tried to throw the curve that Wayne had taught him the summer before. The batter had to jump out of the way. Wayne raised his head and gave Ronnie a dirty look. Then he called out to Jim, "Did he?" Jim nodded his head. After the game Wayne picked Ronnie up by his ears and head, raising him to eye level. "Don't you ever do that again," and then kicked him in the pants. Ronnie knew Wayne meant business and didn't throw a curve again until his dad said it wouldn't hurt his throwing arm.

One day Wayne told Pat Connors how homesick he had been at Utah State. Pat had a great idea: they could attend the University of Montana together. Wayne talked to Montana's athletic department and the basketball coach, Ron Nord. They offered him a full-ride scholarship.

Wayne Estes: A Hero's Legacy

Although Wayne felt loyalty to Andersen and his USU teammates, he kept thinking about the advantages of playing close to home. After a few days, Wayne went to his dad to discuss what he should do. "You'll have to make your own decision, son."

"But what would you do, Dad?"

"I'd go with Utah State. LaDell's been good to you. He even came up here again this summer. Besides, they're the ones who wanted you when no one else did. But you know Mom and I will support you no matter what you decide."

"Well, Dad, I really want to go back to Utah State, but I thought you might want me to stay close to home. I'm glad that we think alike."

With that decision made, Wayne then tried to talk Jim into going to Utah State. But Jim realized they wouldn't see much of each other when basketball started, and he decided to stay in school at Butte.

Wayne continued to spend evening after evening shooting baskets with his nine-year-old brother Ronnie. Some of Wayne's friends couldn't understand his devotion to his family, especially his little brother. But Wayne didn't let their reactions or comments bother him.

Not long before Wayne left for Logan, he went to a picnic with his parents, John and Katherine Cheek, and other adult members of the community. Wayne couldn't stand the sedate seriousness of the group. To make some of the adults laugh, Wayne smashed a butterscotch pie in Cheek's face. Cheek chased him off and on for over an hour but couldn't catch him. Wayne realized if he ran forever, he wouldn't get anything to eat. He called out, "Truce, truce."

"Okay," agreed Cheek.

Suspicious, Wayne insisted they shake hands when Cheek yielded so readily. They both laughed about it as Wayne filled up his plate. Wayne totally forgot the incident as people started getting up from the picnic tables to go home. Coming up behind Wayne, Cheek hit him in the face with a chocolate pie. Wayne kept eating and said casually, "Thanks, Coach, that's my favorite kind."

CHAPTER 6
THE VARSITY TEAM

Weighing 245 pounds, sophomore Wayne moved into 5110A Richards Hall. Coach Andersen assigned him to room with basketball players Joe Warfel, a teammate from last year's freshman squad, Troy Collier, a junior college transfer, and Mark Hasen, a starting guard from New York City. Everyone else on the team lived in fraternity houses.

Mike Casey, whose friendship with Wayne had continued from last year, moaned, "I wish you would've pledged Sigma Nu last year so you could live at the house. You'd like it much better than the dorm. Pledge this fall so you can move in winter quarter."

"Na, the dorm's okay." Wayne hadn't forgotten his experience last spring and didn't want any more to do with fraternities. "Besides, Caser, I don't fit in with that life-style. I don't like all the crap they dish out. And then what would Higgy and Collier do? Do they let Jews and blacks join?"

"They should. I heard the SAE's want Hasen. I don't know about blacks." Casey let the matter drop. Utah in 1962 had not had much to do with the national civil rights movement. College athletes had learned to appreciate minorities on the field or court, but discrimination returned in their personal lives. Wayne was ahead of his time in how he related to people. He treated all people equally. In fact, he developed almost a cult following among the Iranian students living in the dorm. They followed his games closely and regarded him with awe. When he couldn't pronounce their names, he gave them nicknames.

Wayne Estes: A Hero's Legacy

When Andersen recruited Troy in Phoenix, Arizona, Andersen clued him in about Wayne's shooting ability. But seeing him before fall quarter started, Troy couldn't believe that that "heavy" kid could play college ball. However, Wayne converted Troy after several workouts.

Living together at Richards Hall, Wayne and Troy walked four blocks to classes together every morning. They came to appreciate each other's unique personality. Knowing Troy could handle teasing, Wayne started the team calling him "Honkey."

On Halloween Wayne wrote to Jim Furaus. He apologized for not taking the time to see Jim before he came back to Logan adding,

> We play Missoula the 12th of January. Why don't you see if you can make it to the game? How is the Mines (Montana C. of Mineral Science & Technology) football team doing? Our football team is doing pretty good. I think they really have a great team. I wish you could see them play. They got beat by New Mexico by one point, but they should have beat them. They might get a bowl bid. I went up to Bozeman when they played them but I didn't see anybody.
>
> I like this place a lot better this year. There is quite a bit going on. You should whip down, Snuff. You would really like this place. We always go to Salt Lake City. The weather is really nice down here. I haven't seen a cloud for about 8 days. How is the weather up there?
>
> I've been practicing basketball now for about three weeks. The first week was wicked. We had to run cross-country. Wicked! It isn't bad now. I think we are going to have a real good team. I don't know if I'll be first team or not. We have some good guys. One guy on the team, a 6' 9" black, (Troy Collier) is real great. He has as much ability as McGill, but I don't know how he will do. You ought to see him jump. Standing under the basket, he jumps 16 inches above the rim. I've been working him up quite a bit though. Sure!! We go to Ohio the first of December. I guess we will know then if we are any good or not. We are going by jet. I'll s - - - my trousers.

The Varsity Team

Have you been chowing (drinking) much? I've been chowing about every weekend. I'm not proud. It is all there is to do. What have you been doing lately, anything exciting? I've been having a pretty good time. Last week was homecoming. Tonight there was a big panty raid. There are cops all around. Somebody also lit the grass on fire around the dorm. Heck of a night!!

How's school going? Do you like it at the Mines? School is going pretty good for me. I don't mind it, but I'd rather be chowing with all the fellas. I sure miss all you guys. My hardest classes are Physiology and Problems in Human Physical Growth. I'll probably tube (flunk) Physiology. It's the nerts (pits). I'm only taking 13 hours. How many are you taking?

After tryouts, Wayne made the varsity team[1], one of three from the freshman team to do so. He was now an official Aggie. He also started every game his sophomore year. In the team's opening meeting, Andersen stressed eligibility first. "Budget your time and use it wisely. Study hall is for your benefit. Get off to a good start and stay strong. Games, travel, and practice will take much of your time later. DON'T CUT CLASSES. I concentrate on boys who stay eligible."

He warned, "Avoid fights and celebrations after games. . . . I'm looking for players with ability that love to play, very aggressive type players on defense and back boards, smart players, co-operative type—give and take and still get along." Wanting to please Andersen, Wayne took his instructions seriously.

Mike Casey and Bill Puzey, both seniors, didn't get much playing time that year, but they were essential in practice. They knew their roles before the season ever started. Casey appraised the situation, "We didn't resent Wayne. Everyone respected the big kid who worked hard and always hustled. To win you go to your horse, and that was Wayne. Because Collier had the rebound baskets, we knew Wayne had to shoot." Wayne made Gary Watts, the third guard, feel part of

---

[1]The 1963 USU team consisted of Larry Angle, Mike Casey, Ralph Hanson, Kent Jenson, Bill Puzey, Joe Warfel, Gary Watts, and starters Mark Hasen, Reid Goldsberry, Troy Collier, Phil Johnson, and Wayne.

Wayne Estes: A Hero's Legacy

the team although Gary was married and didn't do many things with them outside basketball.

No matter what Wayne did, he got homesick. He talked about his family constantly. Hearing him talk, people got the impression that Ronnie, age nine, could start for USU's freshman team. And knowing Wayne's ability to shoot, they didn't doubt Ronnie too had spent hours in the gym. Wayne wrote Ron, encouraging him to work harder in school than Wayne had done.

I can't wait to see you. Way to go, Ron (after winning the pass, kick and punt competition)! I knew you could do it. You showed them who was best, didn't you. Keep it up Ron and you will be the best athlete Montana has ever seen.

How are you doing in school? Keep studying hard, won't you. You did really good on your first report card. Keep it up! I am doing all right in school too except I'm tired of having tests. Ha! Ha!

Keep it up and play hard all the time. Let me know how you are doing.

Love, Wayne

Wayne's adoption of the LaDell Andersen family, his second family, helped him survive. The other team members never resented this closeness. And it was no surprise why Andersen liked Wayne. He came to practice almost an hour early and stayed after everyone else had left.

Once practices were underway Coach Andersen announced that they would practice throughout the Thanksgiving recess. When Wayne told his folks he couldn't come home for Thanksgiving, Joe used his vacation time to bring Helen, Ronnie and almost everything in the kitchen to Logan. Using their room with a kitchenette in the Baugh Motel, Helen prepared a traditional Thanksgiving dinner.

At practice Wednesday, Wayne asked Casey, "Are you going home for Thanksgiving?"

"There's no time with all the practices."

The Varsity Team

"Well, are they cooking a big dinner at the frat house?"

"Na, our house mother lives in Tremonton and is going home. I'll eat in the cafeteria with the football players who stick around."

So Wayne invited his teammates left in Logan to join him for dinner at the motel. Helen and Joe treated his friends, Troy Collier, Mark Hasen, Joe Warfel, Larry Angle, and Mike Casey, like family. They served themselves from the food stacked on the small dining table and balanced their plates on their laps. They had to climb over each other to get back to the table for refills as they filled all the available space in the room, sitting on chairs, beds, the night stand and the floor.

With Thanksgiving over and his parents back in Montana, Wayne worried about the trip to Ohio State on December first. He had never flown before and he was nervous. The morning of the flight out, he awoke to find three gruesome headlines of plane wrecks taped to his bathroom mirror.

When Wayne saw the headlines, he didn't laugh. "Higgy, did you do this?"

Hasen innocently hollered from his room, "Do what, Wayne?"

"These clippings on the mirror about plane wrecks."

Rushing in straight-faced, Mark examined them. "Oh, Wayne, who would do that to you?"

Crumpling them up as he tore them down, Wayne said, "You won't think it's funny when you have to carry me on the plane. And I'm not scared, just a little nervous."

But the flight went smoothly. Wayne loved the food in flight and offered to finish anyone's meal who didn't want it. He slept when the flight attendants weren't serving food.

This was Wayne's first game as a varsity player. Typical of most sophomores suddenly exposed to the pressures of playing experience and game savvy, he performed in a nonspectacular style. They lost

Wayne Estes: A Hero's Legacy

to Ohio State 62–50. Hasen recalled, "I remember chewing him out—I was a senior and he was a sophomore. He came on strong after that."

The next Friday night, USU took on Montana State College. Phil Johnson, the other starting forward, could hardly breath; he had somehow ruptured an air sac in his lung. Visiting Phil in the hospital, Wayne mothered him, "Philsy, does it hurt?"

Hearing Philsy, Johnson pleaded, "Don't make me laugh, Wayne. That makes it hurt."

"What can I do for you? If I carried you around, would they let you out of here?"

"Na, I'll be fine. I'll stay here and rest for a week or so."

"Well, we sure need you back. Texas Western wouldn't have beat us with you in there."

The next day against Regis, Wayne showed what five games' experience had done for him. His performance broke open what could have been a tense battle and gave the Aggies an easy victory instead, when he rounded up 34 points and set a new school single-game rebound record, jerking away 28. In his seventh game, he made thirteen of sixteen field goals against San Diego State, a school record for a single-game field goal average of .813 for a minimum ten shots.

Andersen, wanting the most playing time out of Wayne, geared the defense so Wayne wouldn't foul out. Not liking the special treatment, Wayne worked harder on offense to make sure he carried his share of the load. He became a complete player. He concentrated hard on what he should do and where he should position himself. Hasen said of Wayne, "I watched him practice free throws. He would shoot the ball, retrieve it and try again. I saw him make 116–118 of 120 one day. He shoots better than 95 percent of the pros."

USU had been invited to participate in the L.A. Classic taking place December 26 through the 29. It meant Wayne couldn't go home for Christmas, the first time he'd ever missed it with his family. Helen and Joe decided to visit Wayne for a week before he went to Los Angeles.

The Varsity Team

They packed up presents and a Christmas tree in a bucket of sand and drove to Logan December 19. They went their separate ways December 23—the Esteses for Anaconda and Wayne and the team for the L.A. Classic.

The team carried a seven and two record to Los Angeles, having beaten such teams as Butler, Regis, San Diego, Iowa, and Michigan State. When asked about the team's success, Wayne credited "Coach Andersen's methods and a great team effort, as everyone can score." By that time, he had scored 162 points with an 18.0 average and had reached double figures in every game except one. He looked impressive for a rookie sophomore. Collier, a fine player, had an 18.7 average and led in rebounding, but everyone expected that much out of Collier. Wayne had felt lucky to make the starting five.

The morning the team left for Los Angeles, seven articles on flying disasters appeared on Wayne's closet doors. When he detected them, he told his roommates, "You guys must spend all your time at the library. No wonder I beat you to practice."

A country boy, Wayne had made a big adjustment coming to Logan, not a big city itself. And while he wanted to go L.A., the thoughts of leaving Logan made him a bit uneasy. He didn't know geography and had never comprehended the United States' size. While flying over the Los Angeles Airport, he asked, "What's the water down there?"

"The Pacific Ocean," Casey told him.

"You mean Los Angeles is on the ocean?"

"Yeah, didn't you know that?"

"How would I know?" Wayne said. "I've never been here before." Riding through L.A., he acted like a little kid. Everything was an adventure. "There's Hollywood! Slow down so we can see some movie stars."

When Casey decided to chance the bus system to Disneyland, many gladly went with him, but Wayne backed out. "What if you miss

Wayne Estes: A Hero's Legacy

the bus or can't find your way back? I think I'll stay here and watch TV." Reid Goldsberry, the other starting guard, and Troy talked Wayne into visiting places of interest within walking distance. As they ambled along, Wayne had a chance to ask a question that had been on his mind for awhile. "Reid, how come everybody calls you Stein?"

"Well, when Hasen's Jewish buddies came to visit him last year, they couldn't ever remember my last name Goldsberry so they called me Goldsberg or Goldstein. Hasen now calls me Stein for short." Wayne used Stein after that.

Competing in the Los Angeles Classic, the Aggies lost to UCLA in the first game, then beat Washington and USC, taking the consolation championship. Wayne only scored nine points against Washington. Finishing the tournament with 49 points and 25 rebounds, Wayne felt good about a 16.0 average against such strong teams.

The tournament sponsors thought he did better than "good," naming him to the All-Tournament Team and dubbing him the "soph to watch." With childlike enthusiasm, he responded, "It surprised me more than anything. It was one of the best things that happened to me so far."

Wayne didn't have time to go home to Montana after returning from Los Angeles, since the team arrived home Saturday December 29 and practiced from three to five on the 31. With no studies, no students, and not much to do, Wayne dropped by the Andersen household on New Year's Eve. Andersen took this opportunity to talk to him and give him some fatherly advice. "You look great! How much have you lost?"

"Ten pounds, I'm down to 235. But it hasn't been easy. I always leave the table hungry."

"I can see it making a difference already." Then Andersen got into the heavy stuff. "I know some fellows on the team drink, Wayne. I wouldn't want to stop them just because their philosophies on life and basketball differ from mine. And I couldn't stop them unless I followed them around night and day, which I won't do. But it will catch up to them. I know how much basketball means to you, and

The Varsity Team

I don't want you to jeopardize your future because you got in the wrong crowd and carried things further than you wanted. Remember the incident last spring?"

"Yeah, Coach. Drinking beers with the guys can get out of hand."

"Wayne, when we travel, you'd be wise to go with the guys who eat hamburgers after the game instead of those who go out for beer. You've worked so hard and come so far, I wouldn't want you to spoil reaching your goal."

"I can do that. I can have as much fun with Stein and Watts and Collier."

After playing with the Andersen boys and eating snacks, they set off firecrackers and banged on pans at midnight. Wayne slept in a sleeping bag on the floor of Clint's bedroom. The bed was too short for him. Andersen didn't have to worry about where his star sophomore was that New Year's Eve.

Andersen held practice at six o'clock New Year's evening. No one complained; they had big games coming up; University of Utah Friday and Brigham Young University Saturday.

Wayne totaled 26 points and cut Utah's zone defense to ribbons in the process. Before the game some Utes had snickered about Wayne's size. He looked like a neighborhood fill-in, someone to put in to have enough players for a team. They remembered seeing his ineffectiveness on the fake and drive when he was a freshman and in early game films. The "fat kid who didn't look like a basketball player" had matured in a hurry, and quickly gained the Utes' respect. With Wayne banging away from outside and the corners, the Aggies forced the Redskins into a man-to-man defense. The Ags beat the U of U in Salt Lake 69–55.

The following day the Ags met the BYU Cougars on the Ags' home court. Most people felt sorry for them facing their two biggest rivals back to back. But they whopped the Y as Wayne canned nineteen points and hauled down eleven rebounds. Wayne gained many fans

Wayne Estes: A Hero's Legacy

during the game, especially USU freshman girls who hadn't gone to any pre-Christmas games.

One of them, Terry Cale, felt a kinship with Wayne since she too was from Montana. Her date, football player Darrell Steele and Wayne's good friend, continually bragged about Wayne and his abilities. Before the game ended, Terry had a crush on Wayne; but she didn't see any way to meet him.

After that game Wayne sat next to Stein Goldsberry in the dressing room. He slapped Reid's back, "If I make it to the NBA, I'll take you with me so you can feed me the ball. You make me look good." Shrugging his shoulders, Reid took off his Converse All-Stars.

A shocked Wayne looked at Reid's red socks. "What's all over your socks, Stein?"

"Nothin.'"

"It's blood. Take off your socks." As he did, Wayne stared at Reid's bloody feet. "How long have your feet looked like that?"

"Oh, I've had problems all my life with my oversized big toes. They cause friction blisters that pop and bleed when I run."

"Do they hurt?" Wayne asked.

"Yeah, it hurts. Haven't you ever worn the skin off a blister? That's all it is. Once I get into the game, I forget them most of the time. See, Wayne, I like this game as much as you do so I wouldn't let my feet put me in the stands."

"But what can you do about them?"

"Oh, I wear mole skin, gauze, tape and try lots of things. The doctor says when I quit playing basketball, they'll heal just fine. It's no big deal. A lot of people play with pain."

Wayne was amazed. He had never really considered the private battles any of his other teammates faced. He felt selfish only worrying about his homesickness and his weight and wondered what other things he didn't know about the lives and problems of his teammates.

The Varsity Team

That night, Wayne went out to eat with Mark and Troy. As Wayne entered the restaurant, Darrell Steele and Terry Cale were exiting. Darrell introduced Terry to Wayne, much to Terry's delight. She made it a point to tell him about her Montana roots. Wayne was fascinated by her petite size.

Monday, the first day of winter quarter, Terry found out she had two classes with Wayne. She tried to get him to talk to her, but Wayne didn't respond much. Terry thought he wasn't interested. Meanwhile, Wayne confided to Hasen he wanted to take her out.

Their next game in Missoula with Montana State University was less than one hundred miles away from his parents and friends in Anaconda. The Montana fans, while still heckling Wayne with boos and insults, admitted he made a fine college player, with his six of ten field goals, nine of twelve free throws, and nine rebounds, something they didn't think would occur during his high school days.

Upon his return, his roommates urged Wayne to call Terry. He decided to ask her for help on homework in the classes they shared since he didn't dare ask her out until he knew for sure she would say yes. As he tried to call her, Hasen and Joe Warfel stood behind him, giving him a bad time. In frustration, he pulled the phone out of the wall. A couple of days later Wayne showed up at the girls' LDS dorm #3. She beamed at seeing him, and it gave him the courage to ask her to go to the movie at the Old Main auditorium that night. Her roommates couldn't believe her good luck but cautioned her about dating friends. She convinced them Darrell wasn't serious about her after only one date. Wayne called her "Squatty Body" because of her diminutive size. After that they spent time together wherever and whenever they could. She sat in the stands with her roommates and the rest of the USU student body at games and made sure she listened to the road games on KVNU.

After road games, Red Burnett, the team trainer, passed out a few dollars to the guys as they left the dressing room so they could get something to eat before going to bed. Early in the season, the beer

Wayne Estes: A Hero's Legacy

drinkers invited Wayne to go with them. But Andersen, worrying about Wayne picking up bad habits, asked the nondrinkers to invite Wayne to go with them. Knowing where he wanted to go with basketball and not wanting to jeopardize his career, Wayne quickly joined the quieter group. The drinkers didn't pressure him. Over hamburgers, malts and fries with the nondrinkers, he admitted, "You guys have as much fun as the drinkers."

A week later, independent (not in an athletic conference) and nationally ranked Colorado State invaded Cache Valley for their annual showdown with the Ags. The triumph gave Utah State the win it needed desperately in its battle with CSU for top regional independent honors. During the game some fickle Aggie fans criticized Wayne as much as the opposition did since he contributed only sixteen points.

Expecting him to score at least 25 points per game, they rode him when he didn't. If he started off slowly, they complained, "Who needs you," or "Let him sit on the bench if he can't hit." When he started hitting, they conceded, "It's about time." While Wayne could understand foes giving him a bad time, it hurt him when his "friends" didn't realize he gave everything he had.

The following Friday, Wayne scored twenty points as USU defeated Denver, a warm-up for Saturday's second encounter at BYU. When he reached the dressing room, most of the team had already showered. "What kept you, Huey?" Troy asked.

"Some kids wanted autographs, and then they asked me for some pointers. I couldn't leave until they couldn't stand my smelly uniform any longer."

Trying to teach him the ropes, Phil told him, "You know, you don't have to sign every piece of paper or program a kid gives you."

"Yeah, but I couldn't turn any of those kids away. How would you feel if your hero signed everyone's program but yours and then said he had to go? Besides, what do I have to do after the game anyway?"

The Varsity Team

"You'll make a great dad," Casey teased.

"I hope so. I want ten."

Traveling to Provo early the next morning, the team worked out in the fieldhouse before eating their pregame meal. They returned to a cramped motel room for several hours before tip-off. The guys didn't ask Wayne to join the card game since they knew he couldn't concentrate on anything but the game. In Ohio and Los Angeles, they had given him a bad time about watching afternoon cartoons. Now all they wanted him to do was sleep or watch "Looney Toons," so he wouldn't bug them by pacing the crowded room, anxious for the game. He admitted, "I get pretty nervous before a game, but after the opening tip-off I settle down."

As the team warmed up, BYU students dressed as farmers marched around with a sign reading, "We've got a mortgage on the farm. Tonight we collect." But in the frantic duel, the Ags defeated the Cougars by three, partly because the Y didn't have an answer for Wayne, who got 25 points.

Monday, Wayne had more to cheer about than beating BYU. Standing on the scales, Wayne yelled, "225! Can you believe that? I weigh 225. I've lost twenty pounds since we started practicing in October. Did you ever think I'd be so slim and trim? Think I need smaller trunks? I'd hate for them to fall down during a game."

Andersen, Ev Sorenson, trainer Red Burnett, and everyone else made a big deal about it. They knew how hard he had worked to lose the weight and how much discipline it took. When people asked him how he did it, he told them: "Mom stopped sending me homemade cookies."

They beat the University of Utah and Montana in a row. Now with a seventeen and three record, everyone prepared for the rematch against Texas Western in El Paso.

In that game Wayne carried an added burden when Collier fouled out with 3½ minutes left. Wayne took matters in his own hands with

Wayne Estes: A Hero's Legacy

Utah State down by twelve with little time remaining. He shot five straight hooks, and as the buzzer sounded, they trailed by two.

The team didn't make a sound for thirty minutes after they entered the dressing room. As they headed for the bus, Wayne took the blame for losing and apologized to the team for not doing more.

Andersen then announced to the team, "We've decided to take you to Juarez tonight for an hour or so. You probably couldn't go to sleep anyway."

Wayne asked, "What's Juarez?"

Bill Puzey shook his head in disbelief, "A town in Mexico."

"Are we really going to Mexico? How long will it take?"

Wayne didn't know any more about geography in this part of the country than he had in Los Angeles. Casey explained patiently, "It's a couple of miles outside El Paso. We'll be there in ten minutes."

While most looked at trinkets and souvenirs, Casey, Puzey, Hasen, and Johnson checked out the bars with nude dancers and decided to come back later to have a better look. They agreed, "Seniors only. The fewer who go, the better. Meet at that Texaco Gas Station, a block from the motel as soon as you can after the one o'clock bed check."

Returning to the motel, Andersen told them to go to bed, get a good night's sleep and be ready to leave for Las Cruces at eight in the morning. "Don't think about the loss tonight; concentrate on New Mexico."

In his shared room with Wayne, Casey took off his tie and new USU blazer hoping Wayne would follow his lead and not suspect anything. Wayne finished undressing, and Mike turned off the light saying, "I think we'd better get some sleep. I'm tired and we have to get up early." Mike got into bed with his pants and socks still on. He waited fifteen minutes until Wayne fell asleep. He quietly grabbed a sports jacket—not his USU blazer—his shoes and snuck out.

The Varsity Team

After meeting Phil, they slipped out the back way. Not long after they reached the gas station, Bill and Mark peeked around the corner. As the cab showed up, Wayne strolled up from behind the building. He announced, "You're crazy if you think you're going without me."

While the five piled in the cab, Wayne asked, "Where we headed?"

"Juarez," Hasen informed him.

"What if we get caught?" Wayne panicked.

"Don't be silly, we won't."

When they arrived, the live porno shows shocked Wayne. "That's what we came for," Mark explained. They peeked in several before deciding which one to patronize. But as they entered, they spotted some of the USU athletic officials, who had traveled with them, watching the show.

They quickly and quietly backed out the door and hailed another cab. Tears streamed down their faces as they took the cab back to the motel. "Can't you just see their faces if we had pulled up a chair and sat by them?"

"They would've never lived it down," Puzey said.

The next day riding to Las Cruces, those five giggled every time they looked at each other or any of the guilty adults. But their lack of sleep didn't inhibit their playing that night. They beat New Mexico State that night by 30 points.

More plane disaster headlines appeared on Wayne's closet before their flight to Colorado Springs to face the Air Force Academy the next weekend. He wasn't worried much about flying these days.

At the pregame meal, he ate two steaks, and then took a snack back to the motel. As he tried to rest, he watched afternoon cartoons while eating Skippy peanut butter. He ate it straight, scooping it out with his finger. Casey gave him a bad time, "It's okay to eat it with jelly or honey on bread or crackers, but you gag me eating it like that." Before leaving for the game, Wayne had finished off the jar.

Wayne Estes: A Hero's Legacy

That night the Ags had their hearts broken when they lost to Air Force by one. Wayne lead all scorers with 36 points. Wiping tears away, Wayne took the loss hard and was the last one to leave the dressing room.

They left Colorado Springs late that night since they played Denver at three the next afternoon. They beat Denver University by four. Troy and Wayne scored eighteen each while Phil banged in nineteen.

At the start of the season, the Aggies had set a goal for their team to receive an invitation to play in a post-season tournament. Before beating Creighton at home in March, they received an invitation to play in the NCAA championship tournament as an at-large team. Shortly after that invitation, they received a bid from the National Invitation Tournament in New York City. Andersen responded, "We can accept only one and feel we must accept the NCAA bid." In defeating Creighton, the Aggies had back-to-back twenty-win seasons.

The next week they arrived in Fort Collins for their last regular-scheduled game against Colorado State University. Everyone reminded Goldsberry and Watts, the returned missionaries on the team, "You better find a church before the pregame meal. We wouldn't want you to miss a Sunday meeting."

After CSU defeated them for their sixth loss of the season, they complimented the Aggies, "USU is the best team we've played all season." Wayne, saddled with four fouls, managed sixteen points to match Collier.

They had to immediately put the CSU game behind them as they had to prepare for the NCAA invitational game with Arizona State played in Eugene, Oregon, home to Oregon State University.

Wayne scored the first basket against ASU and didn't let the pressure ruffle him. With Johnson fouling out and Collier held in check, Wayne got going, winning his individual duel with Arizona's All-American Joe Caldwell by scoring 32 points to Joe's 31.

The Varsity Team

A good part of the 10,400 fans thought the Aggies should have won. The Sun Devils never led in the regulation period that ended 67–67; but they won in overtime. The Aggies' basketball season ended with a twenty and seven record. The loss was difficult after a tremendous season. They knew all they had left was the long trip home and turning in their uniforms.

A few days later, as Wayne was walking Terry back to her apartment after class, he stopped to buy a newspaper. He opened the paper, read a few lines to himself and tucked the paper under his arm, commenting, "I guess I'll have to call Mom." When Terry asked what he had read, he repeatedly said, "Nothing." When she wouldn't accept his answer, he opened the paper to show her that UPI had awarded him "Honorable Mention All-American," an award totally unexpected by Wayne.

Wayne's statistics proved him worthy of the honor. He totaled 539 points and hit on 48 percent of his field goal attempts. He averaged 32 minutes of playing time on a team that won 20 of 27 games. He ranked 47 among the major college scoring leaders with his 20.0 scoring average. His season field goal accuracy made him the third best on Aggie record. Fifteenth among the nation's top free throw leaders, he set a school record from the foul line at .838 per cent.

In addition to the UPI Honorable Mention All-American, he was named one of two sophomores to the NCAA Region 7 District All-Star team by the United States Basketball Writer's Association, *Look*'s District 7 All-America team and tabbed by *The Basketball News* as one of the Top Ten sophomores in the country.

After the season, Andersen predicted, "This guy will become one of the greatest basketball players in Rocky Mountain history. He's only a soph now, but he already has every shot and every move. He'll be an All-American at least two years."

Wayne hadn't gone home between winter and spring quarter because of the NCAA tournament, and he was extremely homesick. He moped to Mark Hasen for days, "I sure wish I could go home this weekend, but I can't find anyone going to Montana. Everyone else went during the quarter break. I haven't seen Ronnie for months. He'll have gotten so big I won't recognize him."

Mark suggested, "Call the bus depot and see how much it costs to go home."

Wayne did, but he didn't have that much cash. Mark asked, "Have you thought about hitchhiking?"

"Have you ever tried it, Higgy?"

"Sure, I've done it lots of times. You're not afraid, are you?"

"No, it's just Mom made me promise I wouldn't do it. She'd kill me if I did. She worries someone will try to kidnap me."

"You're kidding! Besides she won't need to know. We could tell her some story about friends letting us off on their way to Missoula and then picking us up outside of town Sunday. What she doesn't know won't hurt her."

"Are you talking about going with me? I guess it would be okay if we went together."

"Sure, I'll go, but will your mom mind if I come?"

"Heck, no. She won't mind at all."

Wayne's Friday classes ended at ten o'clock, so Mark and Wayne headed north about eleven, after throwing some clothes in their gym bags. It didn't take them long to get a ride as far as Idaho Falls. They got something to eat and then headed back out to the highway. They got into Anaconda about 9:30 p.m. Helen cried when they walked in. "Why didn't you call to tell me you were coming? There aren't any leftovers from dinner."

"We didn't find a ride 'til the last minute, so I didn't have time to call. I didn't think you'd mind."

"I'll get something together in a hurry. You must be starving."

Relaxing, Wayne enjoyed the weekend with his family. He took Mark over to his high school gym so they could shoot a few. He talked to the track athletes working out and introduced them to Mark. Mr.

The Varsity Team

Mike O'Leary, the Anaconda High School principal, told Mark, "Whenever Wayne returns home, he always pays a visit to the high school. The kids idolize him." Mark saw a different side of Wayne in the comfortable confines of his hometown. Sunday morning after breakfast, Wayne went to get his gear together as Helen and Mark sat around the table. "What time is this fellow picking you up, Mark?"

"Well, I'm not exactly sure."

"He will come to the house, won't he?"

"I'm not sure about that either, Mrs. Estes."

Helen had had enough indirect answers. "Mark, do you two have a ride back to Logan?"

"You'll have to talk to Wayne about that."

Helen called Wayne in. He confessed they had hitchhiked and would have to get back the same way. Helen and Joe talked it over, but they didn't have enough spare cash for two bus tickets to Logan. Worried, Helen took them to the edge of town and dropped them off. "Wayne, you call when you get to Logan."

They hadn't stood on the highway long before somebody picked them up and took them all the way to Logan. The driver had a heavy foot and drove between 90 and 100 miles an hour. It scared Wayne so much he couldn't sleep in the car. Both he and Mark worried about their safety. They had thought that their size was intimidating enough that they wouldn't have to worry about hitchhiking, but they hadn't considered getting in with a bad driver.

After getting to Logan in less than six hours, Wayne called his mom. She was shocked they were home already. Wayne was still too shook up about his fast ride home to joke about it.

Mike Casey tried to interest Wayne in the Sigma Nu's again spring quarter, but Wayne declined. Mike stopped pushing him. However, Wayne's roommate Joe Warfel and some freshman basketball players,

Wayne Estes: A Hero's Legacy

Kent Hunsaker, Rudy Castrutta, and Mickey Dittebrand talked him into going through spring rush.

When Sigma Alpha Epsilon offered him a bid, Phil Johnson and the rest put pressure on him to pledge. Deciding the SAE's might be different than the Pi Kaps, he accepted their bid. He enjoyed participating in Swing Sing, singing numbers from *West Side Story*, especially when they won the competition. He had always had a good singing voice and had often regretted not joining the choir in high school.

The Robins Awards Committee, university students and faculty who picked the five outstanding persons in ten different categories, announced Wayne as a candidate for Athlete of the Year. He felt good about it but added, "I won't get it. They always give it to a senior football player." He took Terry to the black-tie affair and saw his prediction turn out: Steve Shafer, the Aggie quarterback, won the award.

When the time came for Terry to leave for Boise to go home for the summer, Wayne and Terry didn't laugh. They both shed tears of good-bye and made promises to each other to keep in touch.

Wayne could barely wait for his folks to arrive to take him home. He had a chance to work construction in Logan making a lot more money, but he couldn't stand being away from his family.

Mr. Connors, the Anaconda City recreation director, gladly gave Wayne his old job back working with Jim Furaus. Wayne never contradicted Jim in public while Jim was umpiring, but after everyone else had gone home, Wayne would ask, "How could you do that? He was safe by a mile!" Their friendship deepened because of Wayne's tutoring.

Jim and Wayne had an hour for lunch. But ten to fifteen kids a day would ask Wayne for a ride home in his granddad's old pickup truck, and he always complied. He usually had about fifteen minutes to eat after delivering them. Mayor Joseph Calnan remembered,

Wayne Vernon Estes
May 13, 1943-February 8, 1965
(Courtesy of USU Athletic Department)

Wayne at six months with his Grandmother Estes (Courtesy of Helen and Joe Estes)

Wayne at six months (Courtesy of Helen and Joe Estes)

*Wayne at a year
(Courtesy of Helen and
Joe Estes)*

*Wayne at two with
his dog
(Courtesy of Helen and
Joe Estes)*

*Wayne at three with his cousin Bonnie
(Courtesy of Helen and Joe Estes)*

*Wayne's senior picture at Anaconda High
(Courtesy of Helen and Joe Estes)*

Wayne and Terry Cale at the Honolulu Airport Dec. 26, 1964 (Courtesy Terry Cale DeRohan)

Judy Morstein and Wayne taken in Logan, Utah Oct. 1964 (Courtesy Judy Morstein Martz)

*Wayne, LeRoy Walker, Jim Harris, and Myron Long
in the basement of the Union Building
Nov. 1964*

*LaDell Andersen, Frank William, Wayne, and LeRoy Walker
at the Honolulu Airport Dec. 26, 1964
(Courtesy USU Athletic Department)*

Wayne helping run the chains at an Aggie football game (Courtesy USU Athletic Department)

Wayne standing on the sidelines with the football team (Courtesy USU Athletic Department)

*Author's autographed copy of the basketball program
USU vs. Montana State University Feb. 4, 1963
(Courtesy USU Athletic Department)*

Posed shot for basketball program cover USU vs. Bradley Dec. 23, 1963 (Courtesy USU Athletic Department)

Posed shot for basketball program cover 1964 (Courtesy USU Athletic Department)

Posed shot for basketball program cover 1965 (Courtesy USU Athletic Department)

Posed shot for basketball program cover 1965 (Courtesy USU Athletic Department)

*Action against University of Utah
(Courtesy USU Athletic Department)*

Right handed hook against Texas A & M (Courtesy USU Athletic Department)

Rebound basket (Courtesy USU Athletic Department)

*Hook against Utah
(Courtesy USU Athletic Department)*

*Fall-away jumper
against Butler
(Courtesy USU Athletic
Department)*

*Adding points to his average at the foul line
(Courtesy USU Athletic Department)*

Comfort from Coach Andersen after fouling out (Courtesy USU Athletic Department)

Talk during a time-out (Courtesy USU Athletic Department)

High School basketball team 1960-1961
Front Row: Jim Devich, Pat Connors, Tom Greenouh, Wayne Estes, Ace Brown, Jack Schultz. Second Row: Coach John Cheek, Mickey Gee, Tom White, Mike Crum, Steve Clark, Jack Nielson, Sam Ulstad.
(Courtesy Anaconda High School)

USU Freshman basketball team 1961-1962
Front Fow: Ray Minkler, Gerry Christiansen, George Moffitt, Ralph Hanson, Joe Warfel, Del Lyons, Gary Schiffman, Dee Hall. Second Row: David Olsen, Jay Sparrow, Wayne Estes, Jim Mandl, Alan Parrish, John Rambo, Mike murry, Larry Angle.
(Courtesy USU Athletic Department)

Seniors from 1963 team—Reid Goldsberry, Coach LaDell Andersen, Mark Hasen, and Phil Johnson (Courtesy USU Athletic Department)

Troy Collier, Wayne and Phil Johnson from the 1963 team (Courtesy USU Athletic Department)

USU 1963-1964 basketball team

Front row: Kent Hunsaker, Rudy Castruita, Gary Watts, Myron Long, LeRoy Walker. Second row: Charles Buckner, Ralph Hanson, Mickey Dittebrand, Geroge Moffit, Gene Widmer, Steve Jones, Del Lyons. Back row: Trainer Red Burnett, Asst. Coach Evan Sorenson, Graduate Asst. Mark Hasen, Larry Angle, Troy Collier, Wayne Estes, Manager Dick Curry, Coach LaDell Andersen. (Courtesy USU Athletic Department)

USU 1964-1965 basketball team
Front row: Larry Mathus, Mickey Dittebrand, Asst. Coach Evan Sorenson, Charlie Buckner, Wayne Estes, LeRoy Walker, Coach LaDell Andersen, Myron Long, Hal Hale. Second Row: Kent Hunsaker, Steve Jones, Tim Smith, Norm Sieften, Pete Ennenga, Stevr Roth, Alan Parriesh, Aldee Konopnicki, Dave Olsen, Clarence Jones, Trainer Jim Railey. (Courtesy USU Athletic Department)

Accident
(Courtesy of Deseret News)

Ken Rich presenting Helen and Joe Estes Wayne's A Blanket and picture at halftime of last home game of the 1965 season (Courtesy USU Athletic Department)

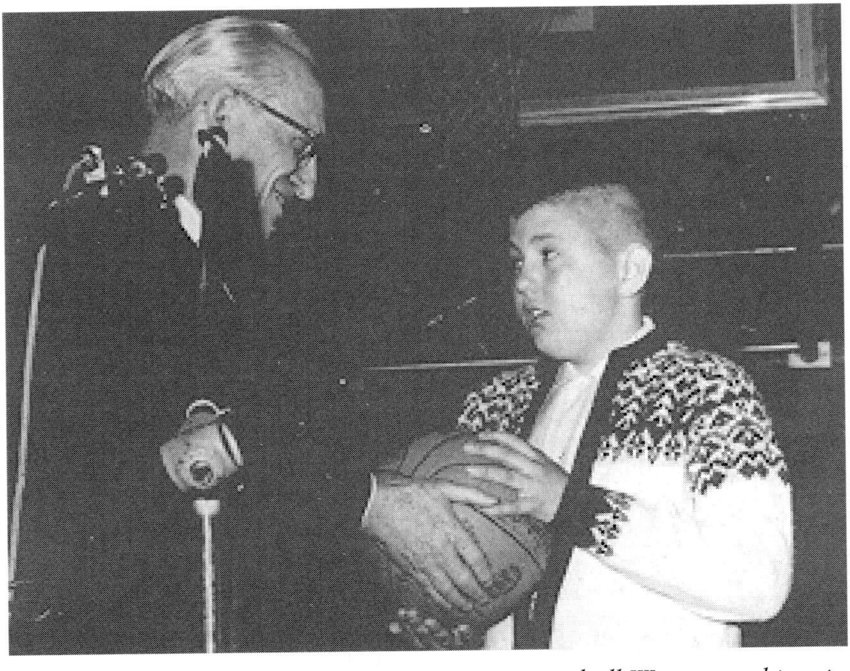

President Daryl Chase presenting Ron Estes game ball Wayne used to set the fieldhouse record (Courtesy USU Athletic Department)

Ron Estes looking at Wayne's trophy case in the fieldhouse (Courtesy USU Athletic Department)

Helen and Joe Estes at halftime of last home game of the 1965 season (Courtesy USU Athletic Department)

Joseph and Helen Estes camping near Anaconda (Courtesy Helen and Joe Estes)

Ronnie and Molly Estes with their three boys: Ronnie is holding Ronnie Joseph, with Brad and Michael in front. (Courtesy of Helen and Joe Estes)

The Varsity Team

"Whenever you saw Wayne, a stream of little kids would be seen following behind."

Wayne and Ronnie slept in a tent in the backyard by the cottonwood trees. They also spent time in their rocky, dirt backyard shooting at their own baskets. Wayne treated Ronnie like his best friend. He was anxious that Ronnie become a great athlete. In return Ronnie worshipped his big brother. When Wayne went to the gym to practice, Ronnie went along to retrieve the ball, giving Wayne more time to shoot. They developed an extremely close relationship.

Loving to hunt and fish, Wayne took Ronnie with him up Morris Creek as often as they could get away. One Sunday, Ronnie, carrying a .22, couldn't keep up with Wayne and his .308. As they rested, a bear lumbered above them. Ronnie begged, "Shoot it, Wayne. Shoot it."

"I can't, Ronnie. If I wound it, it'll charge us. I can get away, but I don't think you can keep up."

"I'll keep up, I'll keep up. Please, shoot it." Wayne stalled and stalled until the bear disappeared from sight, then he gave in. When they went in search of it, they couldn't find it, much to Wayne's relief.

Although busy with summer activities, Wayne continued to write and call Terry Cale in Boise. He talked about hitchhiking down to see her, but Helen forbade it. In July they broke up. Wayne told her over the phone he didn't want to be tied down to someone so far away. This crushed Terry since it was totally unexpected. They had never even had an argument. Wayne told his mom, "She's just too short for me." Terry keep her job in Boise and did not go back to USU that fall.

Wayne's old high school friends had all come home for the summer from many different colleges. Pat Connors, Tom White, Jack Schultz, Tom Greenough, Jim Furaus, Mickey Gee, and Wayne gathered one night to camp near a shallow pond west of town that had deep edges. Wayne and Mickey were the only ones to go swimming. In the water, they planned a trick to play on the rest. With Mickey on Wayne's shoulders, Wayne waded until he couldn't touch the bottom, and then they swam quietly to the opposite shore. The guys on the bank panicked when they couldn't see them. Some moved their cars down to the pond and turned on their lights. Others swam out trying to find them. Meanwhile, Wayne and Mickey sneaked around the pond and got in their sleeping bags. After five minutes when they heard their friends deciding who should go for the police, they came out of their bags and stopped the search.

It was difficult for Wayne to leave his friends to go back to school. But, knowing they too would leave for college made it possible for him to pack his gear and head back to Logan.

CHAPTER 7
AIMING HIGH, 1963-1964

While at home, Wayne received his form letter from Coach Andersen stating Andersen's hopes and desires for the coming season and encouraging Wayne to keep in shape and buckle down with school work. "We want a berth in the NCAA or the NIT." Wayne was excited for the new year to get underway then.

When Wayne arrived, Andersen assigned him to 612 Bullen Hall with Rudy Castruita, Myron Long, and Mickey Dittebrand, sophomores from the freshman team; LeRoy Walker, a junior college transfer, and Troy Collier.

Troy, a fastidious student, was the first one out of bed every morning about seven. Every day he had to prod LeRoy and Wayne awake. Wayne would stay in bed until the last possible second that he could and then hurry to the shower, although he had already taken one before going to bed. His roommates teased him for showering three and four times a day, but he hated feeling sweaty or dirty.

Because Bullen Hall had cooking facilities, they could fix their meals, but that took too much time and organization. They opted for the easy way—eating in the Union Building cafeteria. When they had a little extra money, they walked to a pizza place or borrowed a car to go downtown.

One Thursday night, after looking the selection over at the UB cafeteria, the group went downtown to the New Grand View Cafe for Chinese food. While eating, a ten-year-old boy limped past them

Wayne Estes: A Hero's Legacy

several times on his way to the jukebox. Wayne asked him, "What happened to your wheel?"

"I hurt it playing basketball."

"Oh, who do you play for?"

"The Celtics, a Little League team in Ogden."

"That's great. I play basketball too."

"I know. You're Wayne Estes. My sister loves you. Do you want to come meet her and my mom and dad?"

"Sure." When only Wayne stood up, he told Myron and LeRoy to come. The young boy glowed as Wayne walked to his table. The sister blushed when her brother announced to everyone, "I told him you love him." Wayne just smiled.

Wayne's kindness to his young fans was becoming almost legendary around Logan. He chatted with any youngster who wanted to talk. When a boy or girl would write requesting an autograph, Wayne went to the sports information director's office, signed a publicity photograph, and often wrote a two-page letter to the youngster. At practices, the stands were full of kids who watched their hero in action. He also would hand out game tickets to them. He told a friend once, "They remind me of Ronnie. And I wouldn't want anyone turning him away." Sometimes they would stand across the street from his apartment at Bullen Hall and call his name. He always acknowledged them. But Wayne was not conscious of the big nice-guy image he was creating.

Andersen gave a pep talk to the new team[1] after tryouts. His catch phrase for them was "Harmony promotes power." Then Assistant Coach Evan Sorensen and Mark Hasen, now a graduate assistant, weighed, measured, and tested each player. Wayne stood 6' 6", weighed 235 pounds, with a spread of 6' 9" from finger to finger with arms outstretched, and could leap straight up 23 inches as compared

---

[1] The 1964 USU team consisted of Charlie Buckner, Rudy Castruita, Mickey Dittebrand, Ralph Hanson, Kent Hunsaker, Steve Jones, Del Lyons, George Moffitt, and Gene Widmer with starters Larry Angle, Troy Collier, Gary Watts, Myron Long, and Wayne.

Aiming High, 1963-1964

to LeRoy's 34. He finished last in the speed test at 7.5 seconds, had a jump reach of 10' 5" and a standing reach of 8' 6".

Sizing himself up, Wayne remarked, "I don't think my height is any disadvantage unless I defend smaller guys, but sometimes my weight slows me down." With that remark, Andersen reminded Wayne, "You will lose ten pounds as soon as possible, won't you?"

"Yeah, Coach. Do you want Mom to send you cookies instead of me?"

His roommates, however, didn't like that idea much as they enjoyed Helen's packages as much as Wayne did. She always sent enough to feed the entire apartment. Helen still thought one of the main ways to show Wayne her love was to feed him.

The second weekend in October, Terry Cale came from Boise to attend a football game. She wanted to see Wayne, but she was afraid he didn't want to see her. As she walked into the stadium, she saw Wayne standing on the sidelines ready to run the chains. One of Wayne's friends encouraged her to call him. She did and they spent the rest of the weekend together. After that she came to Logan as many weekends as she could.

Class work went on as usual for Wayne. Lois Downs, a physical education instructor, had Wayne in several of her methods classes. One class mixed PE majors (which Wayne and many of his teammates and friends on the football team were) and future elementary teachers. The intent was to instruct both groups how to teach others the techniques of team sports. The class was an odd mix of women of all sizes mixed with huge football and basketball players. And some of the athletes were less than compassionate about the women's abilities.

Sometimes the male classmates said things to each other like, "Did you see that skinny girl throwing the softball? She couldn't get it to first base in three bounces," or "It took that other girl a whole minute to run forty yards." Wayne would interrupt, "Knock it off. How would you like it if people laughed at you in a math or reading class? If we

Wayne Estes: A Hero's Legacy

don't help them, they might not teach sports to the kids in their classes. I wouldn't want that to happen."

Wayne enjoyed being the tutor in this situation. He would demonstrate how to throw a softball, take their arm, guiding them through the action, then let them try it. "Hey, that's good."

The professors at USU liked Wayne. Some athletes expected teachers to treat them deferentially, but Wayne didn't ask for favors. He didn't expect them to know who he was or treat him special because he could put a ball through a hoop. He came to class on time and didn't offer excuses for his work. At the first of the quarter he checked with his professors to see how they wanted him to handle his road game absences. He took some tests early and some as soon as he returned. When professors offered to let him take a test with him on the road, he declined. He knew he couldn't concentrate on anything but the game.

On November 22, the day before Utah State played their rival University of Utah in football, Wayne joined the noon pep rally in the Union Building. Just before it started, word came over the television that President John Kennedy had been assassinated. The pep rally abruptly ended, and students went silently home.

Wayne took Kennedy's death hard. Running the chains the following day, a solemn Wayne stood numbly on the sidelines. He was quiet for days afterwards. Like the rest of the nation, he was shocked and saddened that someone was capable of killing the President.

But Wayne couldn't continue his personal grieving forever. The opening basketball game was the following Saturday on November 30. The Aggies romped past Loyola. Wayne compiled 37 points, a new high for him, with twelve of eighteen from the field and thirteen of fourteen from the free throw line besides pulling down nineteen rebounds. He led the attack that broke open a tight game midway through the second half. In addition, he tied a school record of eleven consecutive foul shot conversions before missing one.

Aiming High, 1963-1964

Two days later playing against Fresno State, he mustered nine points and nine rebounds in the first seventeen minutes before twisting his ankle. Before Wayne left the floor, he tried to ease Andersen's mind. "Coach, don't worry about a break. I've got strong ankles. I never taped them in high school or here. Don't worry." The X rays proved Wayne right though he did have a severe sprain. With eight days to recover, he felt sure he could play against Texas A & M.

Utah State blasted Texas A & M in Logan. Wayne made sixteen of 24 field goal attempts and nine of eleven free throws for 41 points, 33 in the first half. In one stretch in the first half, he took eleven shots making ten. The Texas Aggies blocked the other one. With that kind of shooting, Texas abandoned its zone defense and played Wayne close, which resulted in a foul and a three-point play. Wayne didn't play much the second half; Andersen put in the subs who needed experience.

Three days later, Wayne took two final exams early before he left for Omaha and Ames to play Creighton University and Iowa State University, respectively. As the buzzer sounded in regulation play, with the Aggies up by two, a Creighton player, flat on his back, flipped in a ten-foot shot. One official ruled the game-ending whistle had blown before the shot. However, after a conference, the refs decided to count the basket. The Ags lost in overtime over that disputed call. Wayne ended up with fourteen rebounds and 21 points, despite the tremendous blanket the Jays put on him. Two nights later, the Iowa State Cyclones defeated the Ags, although Wayne lead all scorers with 25.

Returning to Logan, Wayne decided his apartment needed a Christmas tree. He and his roommates took a bare Christmas tree from the Union Building and dragged it through the snow to his apartment at Bullen Hall. UB officials easily followed the trail to his door. Since the regular students had gone home, USU was a sort of ghost campus. They made him bring the tree back. They needed to use it for a New Year's Eve party at the UB. Wayne rationalized, "We enjoyed it for an hour or so."

Wayne Estes: A Hero's Legacy

Sunday Wayne learned his family was coming to Logan Monday to watch him play four games during the Christmas vacation. He warned his mom, "Don't come in the gym if we're sitting around talking. The language might not be good after two road losses." When the Esteses arrived, Helen stood outside until Ron and Joe checked to see where Wayne was. When she walked into the gym, Wayne ran the full length of the court in front of his teammates to give his mother a hug.

The Aggies, returning home to a friendly court, defeated New Mexico State, University of Arizona, and Bradley before Christmas. Wayne scored 35, 27, and 16 in the three games, pulling down a total of 43 rebounds, to the delight of his parents and Ronnie.

For the fourth game, sports experts didn't expect the Aggies to stay close to Ohio State, much less come away with a win. For most of the night, the Logan fans witnessed as tight a ball game as they had ever seen.

Wayne had a frustrating beginning, but once he got a couple of buckets under his belt, he oozed confidence and points. He hit fourteen of 23 from the field and twelve of fourteen from the foul line besides getting 21 rebounds to lead the win.

His total points of 40 overshadowed that of Gary Bradds, Ohio State's All-American candidate, who had 27 points. At the conclusion, the Aggies, minus Larry Angle who sprained his ankle, carried Wayne off the court on their shoulders.

Following the win, Pat Connors, who had come down to Logan to watch Wayne play, bragged, "You made Bradds look sick."

Wayne made an off-hand comment, "He was kinda skinny," and then changed the subject. The next day an excited Wayne left for home.

Earlier in December, a tall, gorgeous freshman brunette from Burley, Idaho, named Paula Bandy, had finagled an introduction to Wayne through his teammate LeRoy. Wayne felt some disloyalty to

Aiming High, 1963-1964

Terry but could not deny an immense attraction to Paula. Because of the hectic playing schedule, he didn't think much about her until he came back to Logan for winter quarter the night before registration. He looked in the registration catalogue to see when the B's registered. He wanted to make sure he just happened to run into her.

Paula loitered at registration, realizing the E's wouldn't start for another half hour. She spent more time looking for Wayne than picking up class cards. When she spotted him, he was watching her. They headed toward each other. "Paula, what happened to your leg? You're limping."

"I was skiing and hit a mogul and crashed. My stupid bindings didn't release so I tore some cartilage and split my knee cap. The doctor says it'll take weeks to heal. How was your vacation? What are you talking this quarter?"

"Some education and PE classes. I don't want to take anything else, but I guess I have to. Sometimes I wish I didn't have to go to classes and could play basketball all day long."

"But what about your social life?"

"I'd find time to work that in."

Paula had not been an avid basketball fan during the Aggies pre-Christmas games, but meeting Wayne changed that. Monday she saw him in action with 6,140 loyal boosters as the Aggies beat the University of Utah for their eighteenth straight home victory. Wayne manned the backboards with strength going over his thirteen rebound average for fifteen. He also topped all scorers with 28 points, keeping up his 27.8 average.

Wednesday he asked Paula, "Do you want to sit behind the bench if I can get you a ticket for the Air Force game?"

Paula was not really aware of what an honor had been bestowed upon her but sensed it was probably a big deal if it required Wayne to get her the ticket. Sitting behind the bench, Paula watched Wayne break loose in the second half for twenty points. He ended with seven of thirteen field goals and eleven of thirteen free throws for 25 points.

Wayne Estes: A Hero's Legacy

After the game kids mobbed him, and he didn't disappoint them. Paula had to wait her turn with the rest of his fans to congratulate him on a great game.

Before the team left for the game with the University of Montana at Missoula, Wayne wanted to practice shooting a few extra free throws. Knowing Montana would have a good crowd watching their home state product, he wanted to look good for his family and the other Anaconda fans who would come to cheer for him. He asked Gary Watts, a fellow teammate, if he would like to have a contest shooting free throws. Gary agreed. Each would shag the ball for the other until he missed. That night Gary thought he would never get his turn. Wayne shot 65 straight before missing.

The morning of the game in Missoula, Wayne and Troy went shopping, buying white hats to go with their USU blazers. They strutted around town, trying to act the part of big "jocks." Many of Wayne's friends and supporters, who had driven over from Anaconda in the early afternoon so they could visit with Wayne, met at the Dungeon Bar. Wayne and Troy joined them but turned down the offers of beer.

In the dressing room, Wayne asked Andersen if Ronnie could sit on the end of the bench. Without hesitating Andersen said yes and made a special point of greeting Ronnie, now age ten.

For the first few minutes of the game, it looked as if the Ags couldn't handle the fired-up Montana Grizzlies. The Montana fans, except the group from Anaconda, tried their best to distract Wayne with their booing and catcalling. They called him "Baby Huey," knowing he didn't like it. Their strategy seemed to work as Wayne went four minutes and 45 seconds before he hit a free throw and over six minutes before he made his first field goal. One time the ref made three or four traveling calls in a row on Wayne.

Then he found his range, pouring them in despite the Grizzlies' two and three-timing efforts. He silenced the crowd with his set shots. He ended the half with 21 points. The Grizzly fans, not able to agitate

Aiming High, 1963-1964

Wayne any longer, were now angry at Wayne's buddies from Anaconda, who sat in the student section and were cheering for him.

By the game's end, Wayne had made fifteen of 25 field goal attempts, twelve of thirteen free throws, grabbed sixteen rebounds and scored a fieldhouse record of 42 points.

After his performance Wayne confided to reporters, "It gave me a big thrill since many Montana people said my weight would stop me from becoming a college basketball player. Dropping my weight has helped my quickness a lot. I get my shots off quicker and I've improved my jumping and rebounding. I just feel a lot better all around. I get more time to shoot because of Troy's ability to hit from the inside."

Sitting on the locker room bench next to Ronnie and his dad after his teammates had left, Wayne unwrapped his taped ankles. A Montana fan walked in. Wayne looked up, asking, "Do you want something?"

"Yeah. Are you Wayne Estes?"

"Yeah."

"I was sent in to whip you."

Wayne calmly stood up, "You'd better get started." Unsure of what to do, the guy shook Wayne's hand and walked out. Joe Estes was proud that he had taught his son to keep a cool head under fire on or off the court. This was one time of many that that calmness came in handy during his athletic career.

The following week, just before the Colorado State game, Wayne weighed in at 225 and vowed to Coach Andersen that he wouldn't gain it back again. His weight loss had given him a wider variety of shots and he was much quicker. He didn't want to give those advantages up.

That Friday Wayne, remembering last year's loss, banged in 29 points and pulled down sixteen rebounds against Colorado State, overpowering them by five. The following night, BYU invaded the George Nelson Fieldhouse, losing 105–90 as Wayne led all scorers

Wayne Estes: A Hero's Legacy

with 28 including ten of ten free throws. He received great help from the other starters, especially after fouling out with 6½ minutes left.

That weekend Wayne had other worries. Terry had come down to visit, and he finally had to face the dilemma he had created. He explained to her that he had met another girl he was really interested in and had started to date. Terry was devastated. She not only left Logan, but Boise as well. She went to Hawaii soon after to find a job.

Wayne now worried that he had no car and no extra money to date Paula. But Paula didn't mind walking around campus, going to the library, or attending the 25-cent movie at Old Main Thursday and Saturday nights. Taking her back to the dorm at 10:30—the university required all freshmen girls to live in the dorm and be in the dorm with the boys outside by 10:30 week nights—he would kiss her good-night, then stand underneath her third-floor window until she opened the drapes and waved. Occasionally when Mark Hasen loaned them his car, they had a real date—a movie downtown.

The last weekend in January, USU played BYU and the University of Utah back to back. Although Utah State didn't have much trouble beating the Cougars in Provo, Wayne had a difficult first half with only eight points. He made his first shot, then missed sixteen straight times before hitting one more as the half ended. The Cougars sagged the middle jamming Utah State's inside attack, forcing Wayne farther outside than he liked to shoot and keeping him off the backboards. He ended the evening 10 for 31 from the field and five for five at the free throw line with ten rebounds. Talk began to spread that his new love life was destroying his game. Some thought he and Paula were together too much, others thought they were fighting. But others knew that everyone is entitled to a bad night now and then.

The next night, gloom hung over Logan while Salt Lake City basked in bright sunlight. Utah had shocked Utah State 84–72. Wayne accumulated 27 points despite the closest guarding he'd ever received. Twice he made baskets from twenty feet when his man had beaten him defensively. He somehow freed the arm with the ball and arched

Aiming High, 1963-1964

the ball in. Setting another Aggie scoring record, he connected on his 26 straight free throw, breaking Max Perry's 22 mark set four years earlier. Wayne hit fifteen of seventeen for the night.

Even though Utah State lost, Wayne gained the respect of the Ute players. Doug Moon, their outstanding guard, summed up their feelings. "He pops off from a low post pick, hits a baseline or goes over the top. His baseline hook distinguishes him as a great ball player. He's a phenomenon from ten to fifteen feet going either left or right. Unstoppable describes him best. He realizes his capabilities—what he can do and what he can't. He works on what he can do. He's in the right place at the right time."

Two days after losing to Utah, Utah State toyed with Denver at home and saw Wayne become the seventh Aggie ever to top the 1,000-point career mark. Scoring 28, making his total 1,022, he connected fourteen of 25 times. Gasps were heard once when he fought for one of his twenty rebounds and met back to back with the hardwood court. When asked why it took him so long to get up, he said slyly, "I was just resting."

In February the Ags flew to Bozeman for two games with the Bobcats. A somewhat lethargic USU squad received a terrific scare before winning 77–75. Wayne potted two impossible right-handed hook shots in a row from behind the back boards, the latter with fifteen seconds left to knot the score after regulation play. He scored the final point, his 29th, when the refs assessed a technical foul on the Bobcat coach.

Playing Montana State again the following night, the Ags had an easier time winning with Wayne gathering 33 points. These two wins put the Aggies' season record 16–3. After the game, Montana fans said the Montana coaches made a mistake recruiting Donny Rae and Kermit Young out of high school instead of Wayne.

A few days later, Wayne hit 35 points, a come-from-behind basket, with four seconds remaining to give Utah State an 85–84 overtime win over Colorado State. Coming through in the clutch again, Wayne scored the last two baskets in the closing moments.

Wayne Estes: A Hero's Legacy

Wayne always wanted the ball in close games when time was running out, and his teammates wanted Wayne to have it. He could get off a shot that fit the need. His almost mechanical scoring, rebounding, and defensive consistency added to his worth. Collier's quick offensive and defensive movements around the basket added to Wayne's effectiveness. Teams couldn't double or triple-team him when Collier picked up the slack.

Leaving the team in Denver the next day, Coach Andersen flew to Montana to attend his father-in-law's funeral. The team promised to win for him. Although the Aggies had easily defeated Denver in Logan, road situations differ. With sixteen seconds remaining in the game, Wayne calmly stepped to the foul line and dumped in two free throws giving Utah State a 74–72 win.

After the Denver win, they received good news from a phone call from the NCAA selection committee. The Aggies had been selected as an at-large team for the NCAA Far Western Regionals to be held in Eugene again.

Learning that Wayne had gotten home from the Denver road trip, Paula, still limping from her ski accident, rushed over to Bullen Hall from Merrill Hall as fast as she could. When she approached his apartment, LeRoy loudly commented, "Here comes the Paula Bandy doll. Wind her up and she limps."

Wayne grabbed Walker's shoulders and pushed him backward threatening, "Don't you ever say that again." His roommates nudged each other and left, even though Paula was not supposed to legally be in the men's dorm.

Seattle University came to town and ended Utah State's 22-home game winning streak with a 96–94 win. It had looked like the Aggies would break away with Wayne's late shooting when he pushed in seven field goals in 8½ minutes, but the Chieftains wouldn't quit. Wayne finished with 25 points. Four days later Wayne, not playing as much as usual, had 21 points and twelve rebounds against Montana.

Aiming High, 1963-1964

With three games left, the team needed another win to make them twenty-game winners. Even though they would play Arizona State in the Regionals, they knew they had to concentrate on three road games: Philadelphia's LaSalle, Washington D. C.'s American University, and Rhode Island's Providence College.

Losing to LaSalle, Wayne felt responsible since he only scored 23 points and fouled out. He apologized and promised to do better the next game. He scored 42 points when they beat American University.

They lost at Providence, despite Wayne's 31 points. Wayne's season total ended at 753, surpassing Cornell Green's 745 of the 1961 team. Again, the Aggies had to bury the losses and start their post-season practices.

The practices paid off. The Aggies nipped the Sun Devils 92–90, winning a NCAA playoff berth in the Far West Regionals in Corvallis. Falling behind at the start, the Aggies struggled and fought hard to catch up. Wayne put on a shooting exhibition, collecting 38 points. The Sun Devils had a big margin in rebounding, 63–47, besides shooting 43 percent to the Ags 42. But the Aggies refused to let down. The win revenged the Ags for an overtime loss to the Sun Devils on the same floor a year ago.

In their second game against the University of San Francisco, Utah State beat themselves. Troy picked up three fouls early, and the team had to go into a slow-down game that put an added burden on Wayne, who only had 21 for the night. The following night, the Ags lost to Seattle, who had also lost in the first round and would not advance.

When the press covering the tournament asked Andersen about Wayne, Andersen told them, "He's a real good boy all the way. He's genuine. There's nothing phony about him. He's humble in many respects and he's dedicated to the game of basketball."

Returning to Logan, Wayne kept his uniform for use in the Olympic basketball trials in Lexington, Kentucky. Wayne and Doug Moon, a University of Utah senior, flew there together. "We talked

Wayne Estes: A Hero's Legacy

jock talk all the way," Moon said of their four-hour plane ride. Those selected from across the nation had one practice before playing on a televised game Saturday afternoon March 28. Wayne, nailing the first shot of the game, got the West off on the right foot and aided them in their victory over the Eastern All-Stars, scoring nine points in the tussle before a large Kentucky crowd. Wayne could have scored more points, but he put the team first.

After the game many high school basketball players hung around waiting for their super heroes to come from the dressing room. Wayne took the time to stop and chat with these young men, going out of his way to sign autographs while most of his teammates didn't even stop to say hi on their way out.

During the four days of intersquad scrimmages, the coaches continually gave Wayne hope and encouragement. At the end of the week, the coaches announced to the group who made it and why. During these kind of tryouts, the coaches looked mainly for those who could score. Wayne realized he should have forgotten about being a team player and shot more.

Wayne wasn't selected for the Olympic team. But he was one of the few juniors trying out, and his shooting, rebounding, and hard work had impressed them. Since he had come so close to making the team, some of the coaches told him on the side that it had come down to him and Mel Counts. If Andersen had been a coach, they would've picked Wayne. But since Counts's coach helped all week, they picked him.

After the scrimmages, Wayne flew home to Montana for a few days. He didn't try to hide his disappointment from his dad. "Everybody was out for himself. I had a lot of open shots, but I fed the guys closer to the basket. They didn't want to win; they just wanted to look good. If I had it to do over, I'd shoot every time I got my hands on the ball. They won't do well in the Olympics if they have the attitude 'every man for himself.'"

Wayne also talked to his dad about marrying Paula and her wanting him to join The Church of Jesus Christ of Latter-day Saints

Aiming High, 1963-1964

(Paula's church). After he studied the church pamphlets Paula had sent, he told his dad, "I don't know how I'm going to learn all this stuff. And what happens if I can't believe it?"

"If you try, Paula will understand."

Not making the Olympic team hurt Wayne deeply, but other honors he received made up for it somewhat. *Look* named him to their District 7 All-Star team. *Coach and Athlete* named Wayne to their All-America team besides picking him as the best player in the Rocky Mountains. He also made the Helms Athletic Foundation, National Association of Basketball Coaches and Basketball News All-America teams plus *Converse Yearbook*. But Texas A & M Coach Shelby Metcalf's comments after Texas Western beat them in the NCAA playoff pleased Wayne as much as anything. "Barnes gave a tremendous performance tonight, but we didn't see anything Wayne Estes hadn't showed us back in December."

That spring Wayne took an elementary physical education class from Professor Lois Downs. She required the USU athletes to help her with the students at the Edith Bowen Laboratory School, an elementary school on campus. The kids idolized him. He loved throwing and catching a ball with them. He sat around on their small chairs, showing them how to play with the things they could best work with.

When his peers asked how he could stand working with kids and people with no athletic talent, he raised his eyebrows at them. "What the ball does for the kids is more important than what the kid can do with the ball."

In April, Wayne suggested he and Paula go look at rings. Finding one they liked, Wayne put off getting it since he didn't have the money to pay for it right then. He talked to his folks, and they said they would help him financially. Two weeks later, he gave her the ring in the early afternoon right before her piano lesson. He was too excited to wait for a more romantic setting. They set the date for August 28. Whenever Wayne's teammates saw Paula and Wayne together, they sang, "Hey, hey Paula, I want to marry you," a popular song at the time.

Wayne Estes: A Hero's Legacy

Since they belonged to different churches, Paula and Wayne decided they would get married in Paula's church. Wayne didn't have a church he attended much. As long as his parents could attend the wedding, he thought one church would be the same as another.

In May the Robins Awards committee announced the finalists for Athlete of the Year. Wayne led the list of Jim McNaughton, Bill Munson, Gary Watts, and Troy Collier. When everyone told Wayne he would win this year, he reminded them that although the basketball team did better than the football team, the committee always picked the senior football quarterback. When Bill Munson won, people said to him, "They won't know who to give it to next year if you won this time."

May 13, Wayne's birthday, had a special significance for the kids at the Edith Bowen School. That was "Wayne Estes Day." The kids took up a penny collection to buy him school lunch and had him as their guest at the lunch table. They also had the cooks make him a cake.

Wayne treated the invitation as if it had come from the White House and stayed as long as the kids wanted to talk basketball. When they presented him a certificate, he got all choked up. "I should buy your lunch. Teachers always learn more than the students."

On the weekends during spring quarter, Wayne and Pete Ennenga, a member of the freshman team, broke into the ladies' Smart Gym through the basement windows for slam dunk contests with its nine-foot baskets. While Wayne could barely dunk the ball on a ten-foot stand, here he looked like a leaper. When they let others know what a good time they had, some of the big, slow football players joined in; and they had rousing three-on-three contests. Afterward they went to the Cactus Club for beer. This became a sore spot for Paula, a non-drinker. But Wayne didn't think it hurt anything.

When Ronnie's grade school ended before Wayne finished his junior year, Ronnie came down for a week. On the final day of school, LaDell Andersen, Wayne, and Ronnie stood looking at the trophy case

Aiming High, 1963-1964

inside the George Nelson Fieldhouse. Andersen pointed at the retired jerseys of former cage stars Bert Cook and Cornell Green.

"If a player is really great, and that means really great, the school retires his jersey and puts it in the case here for everyone to look at. It's the best tribute the school can pay to an athlete. When the school pays him this honor, his memory lives forever, right where he earned his reputation."

Impressed, Ronnie looked up, "Gosh, is there any chance you'll retire Wayne's number?"

Andersen smiled, "There's a possibility."

A week later, Joe and Helen came to Logan to bring Ronnie, Wayne, and Paula back to Anaconda for the summer. While Wayne again worked for the recreation department, Paula lived in Virginia City, two hundred miles away, working as a waitress. There weren't any jobs available in Anaconda. Since Paula didn't have a car, she and Wayne's cousin Judy walked to and from work every day. On weekends Wayne picked her up and brought her to Anaconda. Helen and Joe made her feel welcome and a part of the family. Wayne and Ronnie slept in a tent in the backyard so she could have the other bedroom.

But Paula couldn't stand being away from Wayne. She quit her job after the second week and moved in with the Esteses. She watched Wayne work at the park and shoot baskets in the school gym.

While Jim Furaus and Wayne worked dragging the field or umpiring, they had a chance to talk. Wayne confided to Jim while they waited for the next game to begin, "I want to marry Paula, but she wants me to get all religious and stuff. And if I do that, she'll want to get married in her temple."

"What's the matter with that?"

"My folks couldn't see me get married. I can't do that."

"Well, you'll work it out. Don't worry about it 'til you have to."

Wayne Estes: A Hero's Legacy

But Paula did. Seeing Wayne not interested in her church, she would back off a little; and then he would make all kinds of promises. Paula didn't go to her church much that summer just to keep peace. The day before their engagement picture came out in the Butte paper, two missionaries from Paula's church came to the door. "We heard Wayne wants to listen to the lessons. Is that right?"

Paula called him to the door, asking, "Are you ready to have the missionary lessons?"

"No."

"When will you?"

"I'll talk to them tomorrow. Then he added sarcastically, "Or can't they come on a Sunday?"

Paula remained on the porch talking to the missionaries. Looking her in the eyes, they pried. "Do you know what you're doing marrying outside your church?" After they left, she went into the bedroom sobbing.

She rationalized the next day that marrying Wayne wouldn't be so wrong since he had such high standards and they loved each other so much. She decided to marry him anyway even though by now she had very strong misgivings. When she came out for dinner, Wayne scoffed, "I thought you were going to that church of yours." Although she hadn't planned to go, after his remark, she knew she had to.

At church, the Ruperts, the head of her church in Anaconda and his wife, advised caution, "You're making a mistake marrying a non-member." Paula's LDS Church had taught her that a marriage in the LDS temple to another worthy member of her church meant that their marriage and consequent family would be eternal.

Changing her mind again, she shocked Wayne when she got home. "I can't marry you if you won't marry me in the temple."

He responded with, "Then you can just go home tomorrow and we'll just forget about a marriage. I won't get married if my folks can't witness it."

Aiming High, 1963-1964

Both cried all night long in separate rooms. Helen couldn't understand why Paula felt so strongly about her church and how she could hurt Wayne like that. In the morning Wayne asked his mom to take Paula to the bus station. "I can't bear to see her go."

Wayne took Paula's leaving hard, but Ronnie didn't mind at all. Wayne had neglected Ronnie to please Paula, who hadn't always wanted his little brother tagging along. Sometimes taking Helen's car to pick Wayne up from work, Paula wouldn't let Ronnie come. He couldn't understand why they wanted to be alone.

As Wayne tried to forget about Paula, things still didn't go well for Ronnie. One day he stopped at the Commons where Wayne sat in the stands with a girl on each side of him. Seeing Ronnie's large Coke, Wayne begged for a drink.

"No, you'll give it to them, and I won't have any left."

"No, I won't share. Please, Ronnie, I'm really thirsty."

Ronnie gave in. Wayne took a big gulp, and before he could give it back, one of the girls took the Coke. Ronnie started yelling. When Wayne handed the cup back to Ronnie, he threw it as hard as he could all over Wayne and then ran home. He informed his mother, "I don't care if I ever see Wayne again, and I'm not going to talk to him ever."

Helen reasoned with him. "Honey, remember in a couple of weeks Wayne must go back to Logan and you can't talk to him or see him very often. You should think about not talking to him again. I don't want you to be sorry later." In a matter of days, Ronnie forgot the whole incident.

Shortly after that, Judy Morstein entered Wayne's life. She had graduated from Butte High School in 1961, the same year Wayne graduated from Anaconda High. Hearing and reading about Wayne during their high school days, she hadn't kept up on his accomplishments because of her involvement in her own sport—speed skating. She had made the 1964 Olympic speed skating team which required

Wayne Estes: A Hero's Legacy

hours of work every day. She didn't have time to watch other sports or athletes.

Judy did take time out to enter the Miss Montana Centennial Contest. As the queen, she rode in the Anaconda Days parade not long after Paula had gone back home. After the parade the city officials invited Judy to lunch. As they walked from the end of the parade route to the restaurant, Wayne and some of his friends walked toward them. He smiled at her and said, "Hi."

An official made the introductions. "This is Judy Morstein. She competed with the Olympic speed skating team last year." Wayne took a second look at her, impressed with the work he knew that required.

After visiting for a minute or two, Wayne offered an invitation, "Why don't you join us later this evening? Some us are going to the park, and you'd be more than welcome there."

"Thanks, I'll see how things go," she replied knowing she would look ridiculous in a park with her tiara and formal. But she didn't have a change of clothes with her.

When she called him to say she couldn't come that night, he had already left. Judy explained to Helen, "Wayne invited me to join a group of them this evening at the park, but I'm still in my formal so I think I better head for home. But I'd love to hear from him." She left her phone number and waited for a phone call.

That week, Wayne called Paula in Burley to inform her that he was reading *A Marvelous Work and a Wonder*, one of the church books she had left. "I want to work things out. I miss you already."

A thrilled Paula encouraged, "Keep studying." After that they called each other frequently. They agreed not to mention marriage until they could talk about it in person.

Judy, not knowing about Paula, called Wayne when he hadn't called her after a week. This time he answered the phone. He asked her out, and their friendship began. On their first date, after talking

Aiming High, 1963-1964

about her skating, she asked, "What do you do?" Knowing he had excelled in football, basketball, track, and baseball while in high school, she wasn't sure which he had chosen to pursue in college.

He casually answered, "I play basketball." Later, as their relationship developed, they laughed over her naivete.

For the rest of the summer, Judy watched Wayne practice in the Anaconda High gym and occasionally played against him. Being an athlete herself, she appreciated his hard work and dedication.

When she brought her sister Penny, they played Wayne and anyone else who dared take them on. He told Pat Connors, "Paula would never do anything like that. I like dating a girl who can get out and play and not worry about messing up her hair or getting beat."

"But do you love her like you did Paula?"

"I really like Judy, but my feelings are different for her. She's my pal. I don't have romantic feelings for her, at least not yet. Mom says that will come."

One Saturday Wayne took Judy to Silver Lake to fish. "You can see the fish easy where the flume lets the water into the lake. I always catch them with my bare hands." When they arrived, he tried and tried but didn't catch anything with his hands or a fishing pole, for that matter. To Judy's knowledge, he never did catch fish bare handed, but that didn't stop him from telling about it often.

Another weekend, Wayne took Judy hunting in the hills above Anaconda. As they walked and walked, she kept up easily. That impressed him. Carrying her gun with it pointed down, she accidentally pulled the trigger. It went off, barely missing her foot. After Wayne's initial concern, he imitated her look of shock the rest of the day.

As they roamed the hills, they discussed Wayne's future but never talked of a future together. Wayne was kind and considerate as a friend and did not intentionally try to mislead Judy, but he still had not told her about Paula.

Wayne Estes: A Hero's Legacy

A week before he had to return to Logan, Wayne, Pat Connors and Guy McClellend took a trip to Seattle. One day they visited the fieldhouse at Seattle University. Finding some of Seattle's team practicing, Wayne and Pat joined them. As Wayne destroyed them, one of the team ran to get their head coach. Coming down from his office, the coach watched Wayne for a few minutes. Finally he asked, "Who do you play for?"

"Utah State," Wayne said.

"You're Wayne Estes!"

The Seattle team gathered around as they discussed the NCAA game of a few months before.

After five days in Seattle, they returned home. When Wayne got back to Anaconda, he made arrangements to live with his freshman teammate, Del Lyons. He then packed up and headed for Logan in his parents' second car. As he left, he thought, "If I can become a consensus All-American and get Paula back, I will have all I want." With that in mind, he made a detour to Burley to pick up Paula, eager for the future.

CHAPTER 8
TOP OF THE HEAP

Wayne felt great when he got back to Logan. He looked forward to living off campus in Pat and Jim Weston's basement apartment with Del Lyons, a good friend from their freshman days. Del agreed to do the cooking if Wayne cleaned up.

Wayne and Paula did not get engaged again although they did start dating. They knew they each had problems to work out and personal decisions to make, about each other but particularly about religion. Paula wanted a temple marriage, but Wayne thought it could wait until after they had been married a year or so. When she put pressure on him, he would promise her anything: study about her church, take the missionary discussions, anything. But because his schedule kept them apart so much, and he simply didn't have the time or the commitment to follow through, his promises went by the wayside. They made up and broke up at least twelve times that fall quarter. The emotional roller coaster took its toll on both of them.

Soon after Wayne had returned to school, Helen talked to Joe about driving to Logan. "Don't you think Wayne would love some company this weekend? We could take Judy." Joe agreed. They decided not to tell Wayne. When they walked into his apartment, it was spotless. Wayne's shoes were all lined up on the closet floor, his sweaters were in plastic bags on a shelf. When Helen saw everything so tidy, she put her hand on her hip demanding, "Who told you we were coming?"

"No one. Why do you ask?"

Wayne Estes: A Hero's Legacy

"This place is so clean!"

"I always keep my room this way."

"You never did at home. What's the difference?"

"I hate messes, and at home you always keep things cleaned up. Since no one else will do it here, I have to do it myself."

Judy had a great time with Wayne that weekend. He showed her his other "home" in the fieldhouse and introduced her to Coach Andersen. As they wandered around campus seeing his favorite places, he immaturely hoped Paula would hear about "the girl from Montana." They went bowling in the Union Building with Ronnie, where she met many of his friends and fans.

But the visit didn't help Wayne forget about Paula. As soon as his family and Judy had left, he called her. She had heard his parents had brought his "girl" down with them. She quizzed him immediately.

"She's a nice person, and we have fun together. She was there last summer when I needed someone to help me stop hurting after you left. But I don't feel about her the way I feel about you. We're just friends."

She cross-examined, "Then why'd your folks bring her to see you?"

"Mom wants there to be something more. She hasn't forgiven you for breaking the engagement. I guess she doesn't think much of anyone who hurts me. And I haven't told her we're dating again."

"Why not?" Paula almost screamed.

"When things are definite, I'll tell her. She doesn't want me to get hurt again."

"But I hurt as much as you. Couldn't she see that?"

"Yeah, but you should have decided those religious things before you accepted the ring. You didn't insist on going to the temple then. She can't understand why you changed your mind. She asks, 'How can she care more about her church than about you?' She thinks Judy's the one for me, and she sees how much fun we have together."

Top of the Heap

October brought the beginning of basketball tryouts. Many people had doubts about the team this year since Troy Collier had graduated. Brent Checketts, the sports editor of *Student Life*, predicted, "If Estes and LeRoy Walker have the great years expected, and the untried boys come through, LaDell Andersen's charges could well win twenty games again this year. Otherwise, things might drag."

Unveiling his basketball squad[1] before the newspaper and television photographers, Coach Andersen sounded optimistic. Wayne, in the best shape of his collegiate career, turned out at a trim, well-proportioned 223 pounds. Confiding to the media, he shared his four personal goals for the year. "I want to beat the University of Utah on their home court, break Max Perry's fieldhouse record of 45, score 2,000 points, and make the first string All-America team."

Andersen told the press, "Basketball is Wayne's life. I've never seen anybody so dedicated. He has worked extremely hard at improving himself. He will probably shatter all existing Utah State basketball records this year after scoring 1,390 points the past two seasons. Many athletes are great except when the chips are down, but this is when Wayne is at his best. If for no other reason, this makes him an All-American." He added, "We're counting on Estes."

Just before the Thanksgiving recess, the fans previewed Wayne's last Aggie season in the Frosh-Varsity game. Wayne's 23 points and fifteen rebounds led everyone. Paula wasn't there to cheer him on, as this was during one of their break-up periods.

The day after the Frosh-Varsity game, Wayne received a letter from Terry Cale in Hawaii. One of her friends had written telling her the Aggies played in Hawaii in December. She offered to meet Wayne at the airport and show him around. He answered her that same day.

---

[1] The 1965 USU team included Charlie Buckner, Mickey Dittebrand, Pete Ennenga, Hal Hale, Kent Hunsaker, Clarence Jones, Steve Jones, AlDee Konopnicki, Earsell Mackbee, Larry Matthews, Dave Olsen, Norm Siefkin, and Tim Smith with Myron Long, LeRoy Walker, Alan Parrish, Steve Roth, and Wayne as starters.

Wayne Estes: A Hero's Legacy

I'm glad you're having a good time in Hawaii. I bet it is really great. I am sure looking forward to getting there. It will be good to see you again. It would be great if you could show me around, that is, if you can find time. Are you working? I can't wait to lay around on the beach. . . . I don't know for sure when we will get there. The tournament is the 26th thru the 30th so we will probably get there the 25th some time. I don't know for sure where we are going to stay. I'll try to find out later and let you know.

No, I'm not going with Paula again. I don't think I ever will either. It is a long story, so I won't try to explain it all in this letter. Well, Terry, I guess that is about all for now. I could write on and on, but I would rather tell you about everything when I get there. Alright? I am sure looking forward to seeing you and having you show me around Hawaii. Be good and take care of yourself.

Writing Terry made Wayne homesick for Paula, who had gone home for Thanksgiving recess. He wrote to her in Burley,

To me you are the most wonderful girl in the world. In fact, if I can't have you, I don't want anybody ever. . . . Without you, I'll just be a common average guy. . . .

They started dating again when she returned to Logan.

In the first game of Wayne's senior year, Utah State looked sharp defeating the Idaho State Bengals. Wayne, going practically scoreless in the first ten minutes and sitting out the last ten, finished with 35 points and fourteen rebounds. They won their second game against the classy Butler team from Indianapolis, who couldn't thwart Wayne, high-point man with 33 points. He also wiped the glass clean fifteen times.

Steve Smilanich of the Associated Press wrote about Wayne. "Once considered too big and slow to play college basketball, he has streamlined himself and his shooting, and the changes could give Utah State another winning season. Earlier in his career, the marvelous

Top of the Heap

Montanan was often made fun of because of his bulk and his lack of gracefulness on the basketball court. Now that's all over, and Big Wayne may have the last laugh."

The following night the Aggies registered their third straight victory against Loyola of California. Wayne sponsored a fine show aside from shooting. He handled the ball on several fast breaks like Bob Cousy. Once Wayne stole a Loyola pass, dribbled down court with a man guarding him closely, dribbled the ball behind his back and fired a left-handed over-his-head shot that went through. He amassed 37 points with 21 rebounds before leaving the game with eight minutes left.

Loyola did scare Utah State once. Early in the second half, someone hit Wayne as he drove in for a lay-up. He fell flat on his back with a resounding thud. As Andersen leaped to his feet, his face ashen, Helen, sitting directly behind the bench, rushed to the floor. A spectator behind the bench commented, "I'll bet Wayne hates his mother running out on the floor. I wouldn't get up if I were him."

When he felt strong enough to get up, Helen gave him her hand to help him up. They put their arms around each other as she helped him off the floor to a tremendous ovation. The spectators liked what they saw. "He's something else."

Two days later, the Ags defeated Pacific. The crowd saw Wayne have a tremendous 22-point first half. He almost matched his point output (29) with rebounds, pulling down 25. His free throw pitching highlighted his scoring. As the half ended, he had 24 of 25 for the season.

During the second half, a frustrated Pacific player punched Wayne hard on the jaw just after an Aggie basket. The refs had already started down the court so they didn't see it. Wayne stared at the guy in disbelief, then calmly forgot it, and hurried back on defense. While Wayne could push and shove under the baskets in practice and in the heat of a contest, he never fought in a game.

Afterward he confided to Paula, "Walker gave me a bad time as I walked away, but I couldn't hit him back. What if I hurt him?"

Wayne Estes: A Hero's Legacy

Besides scoring 40 points and pulling down sixteen rebounds against University of Nevada, Wayne extended his foul pitch streak to 24. Playing with four fouls the entire second half didn't bother him as he canned 23 points.

Impressed with Wayne's improvement over the last year, Pat Pendse, a foreign student from Iran and an avid fan of Wayne's, quizzed him, "Is it true last summer you practiced basketball daily for two hours?"

"Yeah, usually more."

"Why?"

"I always remember what the coach told me." Wayne recited, "'When you're not practicing, someone, somewhere is; and when you meet him, he will win.'"

When asked if anyone would ever break his records, he said his brother might in a few years. "Ron's already a better shot than I am and has more trophies."

Ordinarily, the fieldhouse was packed only for tough games, but the Aggies filled up against everyone. The credit went to Wayne, off to the best start of his career, looking like he would become the Aggies' new all-time scoring champion. In the first five games he accumulated 174 points, a 34.8 average. But just as impressive, he pulled down 91 rebounds. He shot an average of 48.3 per cent from the field, mostly from the outside, and hit 34 of 35 free throws.

When Wayne left for road games in the Midwest, Paula went to Los Angeles to march with the Aggiettes, USU's nationally known drill team, in four Laker games and in the L.A. Classic. They wouldn't see each other for three weeks. Paula bugged him about reading some church books, but Wayne countered with the fact he wasn't even going to take school books with him. He did promise to talk to Alan Parrish, who had returned that year from his mission to England. Paula was appeased.

Top of the Heap

Wayne worried about the Bradley team wanting revenge. When the Aggies beat them a year ago in Logan, the Braves' coach, Ozzie Orsborne, claimed loudly that they had gotten "Homered" and shouted "Wait 'til next year." Their publicity director announced, "We're waiting for the Aggies. Last year at Logan, they picked us up with a full-court press. In Peoria, we'll pick them up when they get off the plane."

Bradley tried stopping Wayne, but he banged in 28 points, two for two at the free throw line and 11 rebounds, in a fantastic performance. Nevertheless, the Braves tasted sweet revenge, winning 69–55 at the free throw line.

To keep from getting bored on this Midwest road trip, the team played juvenile games. Riding a bus through the poor parts of Peoria, they would lean out the window and greet an old woman shaking rugs. "Mrs. Parrish, I didn't know you had moved." Or "Mrs. Long, it's good seeing you." "Hi, Helen, can we come over after the game for something to eat?"

Wayne joined right in unless they picked on a heavy-set woman. If they called her Helen or Mrs. Estes, he let his friends know how he felt. "Don't talk about my mother like that." Everyone knew Wayne couldn't stand for anyone to make fun of his mother.

Continuing the road trip, they met the University of Minnesota Gophers from Minneapolis Saturday. Wayne scored 27 points and ran his consecutive free throw skein to 31. Leading the nation in that category, Wayne had hit 41 of 42 charity tosses. Although the big Minnesota team played rough, pushing, shoving and scratching Wayne, he acted like a gentleman. He impressed many of the Minnesota fans with his calm control of a bad situation. Although the Aggies lost their unbeaten status, they picked up friends in both cities. One man even wrote Wayne, "You never lost your cool. More athletes should emulate your example."

Wayne Estes: A Hero's Legacy

Getting back to his apartment, Wayne had a letter from Paula. He tore it open, but it disappointed him. She sounded like she had given up on their relationship.

The next Monday, while garnering 33 points against San Jose, he saw his consecutive foul conversion streak end. Wayne, eleven for eleven and 42 straight, missed with five minutes remaining. That gave him 52 of 54. A few moments later he added two more.

Calling home after the game, he told his dad, "I'm almost glad I missed the free throw. I hate that kind of pressure. I can't think about other aspects of the game."

Thirteenth in foul shooting in 1964, Wayne had told Andersen during the summer that he wanted to become the best foul shooter in the nation. He practiced at home in Anaconda. He shot at least 125 free throws every day during the summer.

That practice paid off. Wayne, number one in the nation in foul shooting accuracy, now had the unbelievable record of 56 for 58—all in competition.

Wayne used patience and concentration on his foul pitches, taking slow and steady aim and then freezing. In Logan the crowd fell into near silence while he aimed and shot. On the road, he was the target of catcalls and howls. But he came through in silence or noise, adding six to eight more points per game to his average.

The team arrived in San Francisco December 22 and stayed there until Christmas night before going to the Hawaii Invitational Tournament in Honolulu. His Uncle Malvin and Aunt Kay took him around San Francisco Christmas day. The rest of the team slept most of the day or walked around the city near their hotel room.

Basketball experts predicted the rebuilding Aggies wouldn't fare well against the fourth-ranked University of San Francisco Dons. Only Wayne and LeRoy had experience. Starting with the warm-ups, rude fans shouted obscenities and called Wayne names. He just worked harder. He canned nineteen points despite Erwin Meuller, a defensive

Top of the Heap

wizard, covering him like a blanket until fouling out. They lost 86–71.

Playing below his standard bothered Wayne, especially since Wilt Chamberlain had come to scout Wayne for the San Francisco Warriors. Afterward Wilt asked him whom he'd like to play like. "I've always enjoyed watching Elgin Baylor. He's the greatest." Wayne felt a little awkward when he realized he'd said the first thing that came to his mind. Thinking he might have offended Wilt, he added in the same breath, "You're great too. But I know I could never be a center like you."

Going back to the hotel, sophomore Mickey Dittebrand, remembering their silly games on the last road trip, yelled out at a woman who looked like a prostitute, "Mrs. Estes, I didn't know you came down to see Wayne." Everyone knew better than to joke like that, but Mickey was trying to lighten the gloom. This was the last straw for Wayne.

Red faced, he hollered, "You might not have a mother you can respect, but I do. If you ever say anything bad about my mother again, I'll beat the crap out of you."

Someone tried to ease the situation. "He didn't mean anything by it."

"Just don't let it happen again." His anger spent, Wayne slumped down in the seat and fell asleep. But by the time they reached the motel, Wayne and Mickey were talking about Hawaii.

In Hawaii, Terry met the team at the airport with leis. Andersen let Wayne, LeRoy Walker, Kent Hunsaker, and Myron Long spend the afternoon on the beach while the rest of the team checked into the Navy barracks at Pearl Harbor. Eating at the Officers' Mess and sleeping in bunks, they complained about the accommodations until they toured a destroyer at the Pearl Harbor Memorial.

Filled with awe, they appreciated the opportunity they would have missed if they had stayed in a beachfront Honolulu hotel.

Wayne Estes: A Hero's Legacy

Rooming with sophomore Hal Hale on this two-week road trip, Wayne revealed a lot about himself. He talked often about his family and his home in Montana. He told Hal about some of his fishing trips and about some exciting, not-so-friendly encounters with grizzly bears. They also talked about the girls in his life. Hal wanted to know about Terry, the girl who had met Wayne at the airport and taken him all over the islands. "Terry and I are best friends." But Wayne also filled him in on Paula and Judy.

Writing to Paula in Los Angeles, he confided,

> *I am having a real good time, but I would much rather be home with you. I've been thinking of you always.... Remember when I told you of all the really beautiful places in Frisco I'd like to see with you. It doesn't even compare with Hawaii. It would be so great to live here. Everything is beautiful. You just can't believe it. If you were here, everything would be so perfect...*

The Ags faced a Marine team and lost in a knock-down-drag-out contest by three points in overtime. The officials allowed the Marines to maul Wayne, but that didn't slow him down offensively as he harvested 42 points with ten free throws. However, these game statistics didn't count officially since the Marines didn't belong to the NCAA.

Things improved the next night as USU defeated Arizona State, which meant they would face Boston College the final night of the tournament. Boston edged them 120–118 in a wild scoring tilt which saw Wayne put on the most brilliant scoring performance of his career, setting a new school record of 52. While the Aggies trailed at intermission, they ripped the nets for a sizzling 71 points in the second half.

Wayne received the Most Valuable Player Award in recognition of his 122-point total for the three games at the conclusion of the tournament.

However, scoring 52 points against Boston College and getting the Most Valuable Player trophy took a back seat to talking with Bob

Top of the Heap

Cousy, an ex-Celtic who now coached Boston College. Wayne had always wanted to play for the Celtics.

When the team flew back to Utah, Judy Morstein picked Wayne up at the Salt Lake Airport to take him back to Montana for the rest of the Christmas break. She had driven five hundred miles just to take him back home. He told Judy, "Cousy came right up and talked to me. He told me, 'You've got great hands.'"

Impatiently, Judy asked, "Who's Bob Cousy?"

He let her have it. "You don't know who Bob Cousy is?"

"No! Do you know who Leo Freisinger is?"

"No, should I?"

"He's the Olympic speed skating coach." Wayne got the point. "Well, tell me about Bob Cousy."

"He's Mr. Celtic. He coaches Boston College. He told me the Celtics won't draft me. The Lakers will. But he said, 'After you've played a couple of years with the Lakers, the Celtics will get you. You're their kind of ball player.'"

Judy wouldn't let Wayne drive her new Datsun convertible. She knew about his trademark, falling asleep in a moving vehicle. He left his MVP trophy in the front seat and climbed in the back seat to sleep. After driving a couple of hours, Judy ran out of gas. Though she hated waking Wayne, she didn't know what else to do. He gave her a horrible time when she softly told him, "We're out of gas."

"Well, start walking. You're the one who ran out; you're the one who will have to get some."

"I'll stay here and guard your trophy while you go. I'm not getting out of this car at night."

"You're the beauty queen. You can get a ride faster than I can."

Before he could get out of the car, someone stopped and took him to the nearest gas station. After he purchased five gallons of gas, the young man brought him back to Judy's car. Soon on their way again, he fell asleep in the back seat.

After Wayne's long nap, they talked more about the trip. Wayne kept talking about the city of San Francisco. "It's beautiful with all those hills. I think I might like living there some day." And then turning to Judy, he asked, "Would you like living there?"

Judy didn't know what to make of the question Wayne had asked so innocently. Realizing she was in love with him made her want to assume his question was a sort of proposal.

Even though Helen had told her he loved her, she couldn't be sure. She let him go back to sleep while she went over his tone of voice and every word he had said, wondering just what he had meant.

Judy dropped Wayne off at home late Friday. Helen spent every spare minute cooking for Wayne. Sitting down to mashed potatoes, ribs, creamed-style corn, tossed green salad, shrimp salad, rolls and cake, Helen would add, "There's potato salad in the fridge if you want some of that." He chowed down on everything for the next two days, eager to please his doting mother.

He called Paula the Monday after he arrived back in Logan before he'd even unpacked, saying he'd come right over. She wanted to talk about "them," not about basketball tournaments or marching trips. She had had time to think about her feelings and their future together. Wayne convinced her that he loved her and wanted to marry her, and he promised again to look into her religion. But after a few days she could see he hadn't changed. Going to the admissions office in Old Main, she withdrew from school and called her dad to pick her up. She enrolled the next day at Brigham Young University, in Provo, Utah, about one hundred miles south of Logan. When Wayne called her, Karen Hill, her roommate, told him she'd dropped out and gone to BYU.

Wayne began spending extra hours in the fieldhouse so he wouldn't have to think about Paula. And that worked until he walked

Top of the Heap

off the court. He couldn't talk about his frustrations with his parents or Del or anyone. They didn't want him involved with Paula after she broke off their engagement.

University of Utah was picked to easily defeat Utah State in their upcoming game in Salt Lake City. Wayne had a terrible first half, scoring only three baskets in eleven attempts, partly because of the pressure George Fisher applied, who glued himself to Wayne.

Utah held Wayne to seven points in the first 19 minutes and 58 seconds of action. The Aggies, thirteen points behind, passed Wayne the ball in an Aggie corner. With two seconds left in the half, since the Utes weren't guarding him, Wayne, wearing a look of distain, turned toward the basket and threw the ball, a shot made in utter disgust at the way things had gone. He hadn't taken aim. Some of the fans in the east stands tittered. After the whistle blew with the ball in the air, the ball swished through the nets. Wayne's two points cut Utah's lead to eleven.

Andersen lit a fuse at halftime that exploded as Wayne caught fire midway in the third period. The Aggies scalped the Utes 86–84 in a major upset victory. Wayne's turn-around spelled the difference between victory and defeat. As the game ended, everyone in the fieldhouse recognized Wayne as the "All-American." He ended up with 32 points and thirteen big rebounds. His two points that went through the net after the halftime gun sounded spelled the margin of victory.

After the victory, Wayne, with tears of joy, walked off the floor; in the dressing room, he bent over, exhausted from the struggle. A reporter asked, "Was it great defense that allowed you only nine points in the first half?"

Wayne admitted, "Yes, their defense was good, but I was just too tight. I wanted to play a good game, and I simply tightened up. I finally came around in the second half. It sure feels good to win this one."

But Utah State couldn't savor its victory long since they faced BYU two days later. While the Aggie team and fans expected to win, the

Wayne Estes: A Hero's Legacy

Cougars out-ran and out-shot them. A tired Wayne proved unbelievable, compiling 34 points and playing a fine defensive game.

While Wayne focused on Colorado State, Harvey Kirkpatrick publicized Wayne for his All-American bid. A photographer filmed him so a promotional piece could be sent to sportscasters and college coaches throughout the country. During the half-hour filming, he didn't miss one shot. Shaking his head, the photographer commented, "I planned on shooting all afternoon. From experience I thought I would shoot and reshoot to make the film look good. That's normal. Lots of people freeze with the camera on them in an empty gym but it didn't bother Wayne at all. He thrives on pressure."

As the film showed Wayne in game action and the staged shots in the gym, Kirkpatrick talked about Wayne's abilities and accomplishments. On film Wayne admitted he practiced free throws just like any other shot. Pictures of Andersen instructing Wayne also ran with Andersen's voice explaining how Wayne had responded to coaching and his great clutch ability.

As the film went out all over the country, Wayne worried about the team. In losing to Colorado State, Wayne had virtually executed a one-man show gathering nineteen rebounds and 31 points. The guys' talk of giving up made Wayne work harder. Tim Smith, a teammate who never played much, kept messing around the following Monday at practice. Wayne, remembering he had settled down during football practices after Coach Williams in Anaconda had gotten after him, held Tim against the wire screen behind the basketball standard and yelled: "If you don't care about basketball, why don't you quit? Don't make it hard for the rest who want to work."

The team headed for El Paso. They lost to Texas Western 68–62 when they should have won. They outscored the Miners by eight points from the field, shot better than 64 percent, and over-all played better ball. Although Wayne worked against a sagging defense that seldom permitted him to get the ball, he hit eleven of fifteen field attempts, made four free throws and gathered eight rebounds. With

Top of the Heap

thirty seconds left, the Miner fans gave Wayne the night's biggest ovation.

The depressed team quietly sat in the dressing room. The coaching staff, to boost spirits and having learned from past experience, charted a bus and took everyone across the border to Juarez, hoping to keep everyone out of trouble. LeRoy Walker, Alan Parrish, Hal Hale, and Wayne walked faster and faster, and soon lost the coaches. The four found this wasn't such a smart idea after they had problems with the language, wound up in an unsavory part of town, and never did get any dinner.

Getting back to the motel after two o'clock, the team slept in the next day and then flew to Tempe for the Arizona State game in the afternoon. Winning eluded the Aggies again. Wayne's 29 points and twelve rebounds wasn't enough. People started asking, not if Utah State would make it to the NCAA tournament, but if they would end up with more wins than losses.

Reporters and opposing coaches who praised Wayne by pointing out his true sense of competitiveness—always down to business while on the floor and always giving one hundred percent—didn't make losing any easier. While he positioned himself in the right place at the right time, remained alert to what took place, and stayed calm and unruffled even when two or three men hung on him, his performances rarely satisfied himself. He remembered little mistakes and went over them in his mind so he wouldn't make the same mistake twice.

Feeling the pressure of two more road losses, Monday's intense practice put everyone on edge. Coach told Dave Olsen, "Play rough against Wayne. Since the U won't go easy on him, he needs that preparation." The subs doubled and tripled teamed Wayne, scratching and gouging him.

Wayne complained as he ran down the court. "Get these guys off my back."

Wayne Estes: A Hero's Legacy

Andersen hollered back, "Don't complain; get in there and work." As the situation deteriorated, Wayne went over to Andersen, showing his scratches. Andersen commented, "Oh, you big baby."

Looking Andersen right in the eye, Wayne shouted, "Bull shit," and went running down the court.

The coach called out, "Wayne, come here." When Wayne reached Andersen, the coach ordered him, "Sit down and think about it awhile." Wayne slumped on the end of the bench, his elbows on his knees, chin in hands staring at the floor. A few moments later seeing him pouting, Andersen suggested, "Why don't you take an early shower?" Quietly leaving the floor, Wayne walked to the dressing room, changed clothes and left the fieldhouse.

It bothered Andersen to treat Wayne so harshly since he knew his teammates had roughed him up on his orders. He started another phase of practice, left Ev Sorensen in charge, and went to the dressing room to apologize to his bread-and-butter man. But Wayne had gone.

Waiting outside Andersen's office the next morning, Wayne rehearsed his apology. When Andersen walked up the stairs, Wayne met him teary eyed to make amends, "Coach, I'm sorry. I shouldn't have talked to you like that."

But before he could get any more out, Andersen interrupted, "Wayne, you were right. Those guys were rough. I'm sorry too." Andersen explained, "I wanted to prepare you for the game situation, but I should have told you my plans so you'd understand. I should have stopped them. I guess I took those road losses out on you."

"It's okay, Coach." They shook hands and Wayne left for class.

The week preceding the University of Utah return match in Logan, Wayne felt as if someone had strapped him to a roller coaster. The initial drop came with the problems with Andersen. Things got better when they apologized and when the Associated Women Students (every female enrolled in school) named him as one of the eight Most Preferred Men on campus.

Top of the Heap

Rhonda Hammond, Miss Idaho for 1964, had had her eye on Wayne since the beginning of fall quarter, but she didn't start pursuing him until Paula left town. The day the women could put in their bid for the Preference Ball, Rhonda made sure she got there early so no one would beat her in asking Wayne.

Wayne loved the attention Rhonda paid him. Because he had worried about being nominated for "Most Preferred Man" and not having a date, the invitation from Rhonda eased his mind. He walked over to Merrill Hall, pushed the button on her mailbox and waited on the heater in the foyer for her to come down so he could give her his answer.

Paula's former roommate Vickie Wankier heard about Wayne and Rhonda and called Paula Wednesday. "Paula, Wayne's been nominated for 'Most Preferred Man on Campus.' And I heard Rhonda Hammond asked him to the dance. Have you talked or written to him?"

"No, and it's killing me."

It will be "Estes Night" this Saturday. Everyone's sure he'll break Cornell Green's scoring record then. Why don't you drive up and see us and him?"

"Do you think I should?" Paula asked.

"Yeah, if you don't talk, you'll never get back together again, and that's what you want, isn't it?" Vickie insisted.

"I'm still kind of confused. I'll let you know if I can come up Saturday. Thanks for telling me. I'm pretty lonely down here."

Wayne was quite disappointed when he realized he shouldn't dance the night before a "big" game—standing around or dancing made his legs tired—and he had to be in top shape for Utah. He explained the situation to Rhonda and broke the date.

His mom, dad, Ronnie, and Judy arrived Thursday. They wanted to see him break Cornell Green's scoring record during the U of U game. That afternoon, when Wayne went to the athletic office with Ronnie and Judy, the secretary handed him a letter. Jimmy Draper,

Wayne Estes: A Hero's Legacy

an eleven-year-old boy from Logan sent an article from *Senior Scholastic* called "Shoot-'em Up Wayne!" Wayne asked the secretary for athletic department stationary. With Ronnie and Judy looking over his shoulder, he stood at the counter and wrote:

> *Jim, you made me feel happy and proud when I got your letter. It was one of the nicest letters I have ever received. Also I would like to thank you very much for the article you sent me. Just knowing that a great little guy like yourself looks up to me gives me a great feeling. I would sure like to meet you sometime and talk things over. We could talk about basketball and maybe I could give you a few pointers. I'm sure glad you like basketball. Just remember, if you practice hard and never quit trying, you will be a great basketball player some day.*
>
> *When you come to the Texas Western game, come talk to me. Don't forget because I am sure looking forward to it. We play the University of Utah tomorrow. It will be a tough game, but I think we can win. I'm sending you this picture. I sure hope you like it. Also, I'll try to get a program and have all the team sign it for you. Again, thanks very much for your letter and I am sure looking forward to talking to you.*
>
> *Your good friend,*
>
> *Wayne Estes*

His dad called the next morning asking, "Have you seen the article John Mooney wrote about you in *The Salt Lake Tribune*? It's great." Reading it over breakfast, Wayne couldn't help smiling.

> *"Baby Huey," barring a serious accident, will devour all Utah collegiate scoring records. Estes needs 18 points against the Utes here Saturday night to establish a career record for Aggie basketball scoring. Andersen's offense is simple. "We want Huey in a position so when he gets the ball he can shoot and score. Huey, something like a strong, rugged Big 10 football team, literally wears down his guards. A lot of time you'll see one of those strong teams held well in check until the second half or even the fourth quarter, but then the strength tells*

Top of the Heap

and the game breaks wide open. That happened against Utah when they held him to nine points the first half, and then he broke away for 23 in the second half when we rallied to win the game," Andersen philosophized.

Andersen said, "Wayne is the greatest because he not only has a greater variety of shots than most shooters, but also, he is a good feeder and rebounder." Did he say feeder? Yes, feeder. Wayne led the team in assists last year, a remarkable feat since he also led in scoring—and rebounding. Estes shoots, make no bones about that. He'll cast off with the slightest defensive miscue. But he's a team man who'll feed the ball to a teammate in a better position to score, and this is a rarity.

Few All-Americans from this area in basketball have earned their laurels harder than Estes. Wayne, a husky young man pounding up and down the courts in the modern racehorse game, has to stay in there all the time, or the offense is cut in half. Still, despite the defensive concentration, he carries a 32.1 average. And Estes hasn't fattened his average against the patsies. Win or lose, Estes, a champion, will ruin the opposing team's hopes if they make one defensive lapse against him.

After reading the article Wayne had other matters he needed to bring up. "Dad, I signed up for a ten-thousand dollar life insurance policy with Sylvester."

"I thought we told you to wait until you signed a pro contract."

"Well, he wouldn't leave me alone. I'd be out playing ball with some little kids in the play grounds and here'd come Sylvester. I finally signed it just to get him off my back. Dad, I couldn't tell L. J. Sylvester no. Remember when I thought he was the greatest when I was in ninth grade and he was an Olympian."

"I can understand that. What's it going to cost you?"

"Not much. I'm young and healthy. They know I'm no risk. And if anything happened, you and mom are the beneficiaries. He even told me you'd get triple indemnity if I die within thirty days of signing the policy. But that won't happen."

Wayne Estes: A Hero's Legacy

Around six o'clock, Joe let Wayne off at the fieldhouse.

That night, in setting an all-time Aggie scoring record, he poured through 43 points, hitting 26 in the first half. He had to do what the Aggies got done just about by himself. The Aggies took some shabby shots and would have done much better if they had fed him more. Wayne and Fisher engaged in a pushing battle all night, juggling for position, which caused some pushing off fouls against Wayne trying for position. This cut down his inside effectiveness and made him move to the outside. The Ute bench, led by the assistant coaches, heckled him all night.

With 2:30 remaining, Wayne left the game with five personal fouls. As he went to the bench, Assistant Coach Jerry Pimm yelled some crude remarks at him. Looking at him, Wayne just shook his head. The Aggie fans gave him a well deserved standing ovation which he acknowledged with a bow. The Aggies lost 111–104.

After the game Helen marched over to the Ute bench, shouting, "I'm Wayne's mother, and I didn't appreciate the way you treated him tonight."

Joe kept pulling her arm saying, "Let's just forget it."

Helen wouldn't let Joe deter her. "Who gave you the right to act like that?"

Pimm laughed it off saying, "I was just trying to rattle him. It's part of the game. Besides who minds a little razzing in athletics?"

"I do." When Pimm offered his hand to Mrs. Estes, she turned her back on him. "I wouldn't shake hands with someone as bush (minor league) as you." She almost spit the words at him as she walked off.

As Helen, Joe, Ronnie, and Judy left the court, one of Wayne's former teammates told the Esteses, "Tonight proved Wayne's an All-American. Otherwise he would have knocked Pimm's block off."

Top of the Heap

After the game Vickie and Karen waited for Wayne to tell him that Paula had come to the game and wanted to talk to him. "I've got to spend some time with my folks, but as soon as I can, I'll leave them at the motel and come to your apartment and get Paula. Tell her not to leave."

When they finally got together, after a month's absence, they didn't argue about anything, not religion or Judy. When Paula left to return to Provo, they had agreed to patch up the relationship.

Sunday morning the Estes family and Judy packed their belongings for the trip back to Anaconda. A jaded Wayne showed up to say good-bye. Whenever Judy left Wayne, she parted with, "See ya later." Even when they wrote or ended a phone conversation, she concluded with that phrase. However, as they were leaving, Judy said "Good-bye." She hurriedly corrected herself, "Not good-bye. I mean I'll see you later." And they left.

Meanwhile in Provo, realizing that they had avoided all of their differences Saturday and hadn't solved any problems, Paula wrote Wayne a twelve-page letter Monday. In it she said,

Wayne, you're not giving the church a chance, nor yourself a chance, nor are you giving me a chance. . . .

It's just like you having a goal to work for so far in your life—that was being an All-American and a very great ball player. You had to work very hard at first and now it's all paying off. You're famous, you feel accomplished and you feel good. But that will soon end. You will have completed that goal this year, and you may complete a pro ball goal in a few more years. But Wayne what after that? What goals will you have that are really truly important in life? What could possibly make you love your wife more than to be working for the same goal she is and to know that it's the right goal and one that will pay off in so many wonderful rewards in the end that you could never regret one hardship at first?

Wayne Estes: A Hero's Legacy

When Wayne received the letter, his heart soared; he felt he finally understood Paula's religious feelings. He carried the letter around for days, telling people he'd never felt better in his life. He would talk to Paula Saturday when the team played the Y. They could easily work things out and get back together permanently. They arranged to meet after the game.

Saturday morning, Wayne eagerly boarded the bus. The team arrived in Provo about nine o'clock.

For 37 minutes the underdog and out-manned Aggies battled the talented Cougars basket for basket, making the Cougars fight for their lives before BYU pulled out the victory. Wayne pumped in 37 points in the first 33 minutes as the Ags managed to lead most the game.

Wayne hit three baskets in a row to break a 40–40 deadlock and let the Aggies hold an intermission lead. Andersen had Wayne stay under his own basket while BYU shot foul shots, which drew a good BYU rebounder with him and gave Utah State a better chance on the boards. The last several minutes BYU pulled ahead, but by then Utah State had four of their players on the bench with five personal fouls. The final score of 89–80 didn't indicate how close the Ags played the favored Cougars.

Wayne thrilled the nearly 14,000 fans watching the game in the fieldhouse and by closed circuit television with sensational shooting. But it wasn't only Wayne's ability to shoot that impressed the BYU fans. Bruce Olsen, BYU's student body president, said of Wayne, "The most impressive thing is his constant control. He never seems to get ruffled and he always remains a gentleman and a sportsman."

Neil Roberts, the BYU sophomore center, said, "I almost went to Utah State so I had a special feeling about playing them and playing against Wayne. Here I was, a little sophomore playing against an All-American. I was, to say the least, apprehensive."

Roberts added, "It doesn't take long to get to know somebody on a basketball court. And it didn't take me long to find out about Wayne. What a great athlete. But more than that, he was such a nice guy. I got a finger on one of his famous hook shots. But it still went in. With

Top of the Heap

Wayne, there wasn't any in-your-face stuff or anything like that. We were running down the court, and he said, 'Boy, I was lucky on that one.'"

He also impressed the youngsters in the stands. Hundreds of young boys and girls started asking for his autograph before he had gotten to the visiting team's dressing room. He took fifteen minutes to sign programs.

In the locker room the Lakers' General Manager Mohs spoke to Wayne. "I flew to Provo just to see you play. You're going to be the Lakers' first pick in the next draft. I've scouted you five times in the last two seasons, and you've got it all. You've got an unbelievable shooting touch."

That night Wayne and Paula worked out their differences. After leaving Provo Sunday, he stopped at KSL TV to do an interview with them. After he finished, Mike Murry, a friend and teammate from his freshman year, called the station to talk to him. Wayne told Mike, "I've got some extra tickets if you want to come to the game tomorrow night. Feel free to bring a friend." Mike jumped at the chance and arranged to meet him at the Union Building after the pre-game meal about 4:30.

Getting back to Logan Sunday evening, Wayne checked in with Andersen to tell him, "Paula and I are back together. I'm going to have the missionary lessons. I won't have to worry about Paula now—I can concentrate on the rest of the season." Then the talk turned to possible records and the game with Denver.

Wayne left Andersen's psyched up. As he looked at the Ags' upcoming schedule, he had five chances to break the fieldhouse record. If he reached the 2,000 mark with 47 points, at the same time he would break Max Perry's record of 45. Many had already suggested that he could get both records Monday night against Denver. He couldn't wait for the chance to play on February 8. An excited Wayne tossed and turned for a long while before he slept.

CHAPTER 9
LEGACY

February 9 dawned colder, bleaker, and grayer. Wayne's death had a sobering effect on Logan, Anaconda, and the nation. People jumped out of bed when their alarm clocks sounded, hoping the bizarre nightmare would end with the light of day.

At the Andersen home, LaDell and Donna hadn't gone to bed. As their boys slept, they mourned. Donna left LaDell's side a few minutes before eight to inform their sons they wouldn't need to go to school. Their hero Wayne had died during the night. After she broke the news, she returned to LaDell who continued to grieve.

Eight-year-old Brian crawled out of bed crying, not quite understanding the reality of it all. Stumbling to the hallway, he stopped at the sight in his parents' room. Both were kneeling at their bedside. LaDell draped his hands around his head as the tears poured down his cheeks. He pleaded again and again, "Why Wayne? Why did it have to be him?"

In Anaconda Judy Morstein went to Helen and Joe. They comforted one another. Neither his parents or Judy had known that Wayne had patched up his relationship with Paula. Helen had still held out hope that he would marry Judy. Because Helen insisted Judy stay with them, reporters from Associated Press mistakenly published that she and Wayne were engaged.

Wayne's peers wept unashamedly as they walked in a daze to classes. They tried to remember only the glory of the game, but the

Wayne Estes: A Hero's Legacy

tragedy of his death haunted their thoughts. When some English faculty members read "To An Athlete Dying Young" to their classes and discussed the good side of a young athlete's death, the students' raw feelings couldn't and didn't welcome cold, intellectual philosophies of death. What they really wanted was to be told the story wasn't true and Wayne would not only play again Friday night but would also have a stellar pro career. And if that couldn't happen, they wanted the minute details of the tragedy that no one seemed to know or wouldn't share.

Many local elementary and junior high teachers had to deal with psychological traumas their students were experiencing. They admitted they didn't have any good answers. They didn't know the what's and why's of the night's happenings either. They let the kids talk about Wayne, the game the night before, his records, his basketball skills, times they had gotten autographs or talked to him after practices.

People in Anaconda were in a state of shock when they heard the news. Some had followed every game Wayne played at USU. Everyone thought about the irony of the situation. So many coincidences had occurred. Nearly to the basket, Wayne broke the fieldhouse record and got his 2,000 points. Some writers said basketball was Wayne's life and that he had accomplished all of his goals.

But those who had already counted on Wayne influencing hundreds of thousands during his pro career with his dedication, decency, and devotion to family, knew Wayne had much left to achieve. His family, friends, and fans put athletics in their proper perspective. Wayne needed the chance to be a husband, a father, a coach, a neighbor, and eventually a granddad.

Wednesday Del Lyons and Utah State athletic director Frank Williams accompanied Wayne's body to Anaconda, the closely knit smelter community of 11,000. Flags flew at half mast; businesses closed their doors.

Legacy

Joe and Helen agreed to have two funerals on Friday, requiem rites at St. Mark's Episcopal Church and a public service a half hour later a block away in the Anaconda Senior High School Memorial Gym.

Over 4,000 packed into the memorial services. Visitors included state, city and county representatives, legislators, and coaches from Montana high schools and colleges. Wayne's high school friends Jim Furaus, Pat Connors, Tom Greenough, Mick Gee, Jack Schultz, Edward Cutler, Michael Crum and Ace Brown served as pall bearers. His college teammates, who had flown in for the funeral, acted as honorary pall bearers.

In the gym, six lighted candles, a blue and white wreath, and a gold wreath that looked like a basketball replica flanked the casket. The Esteses had received over 200 floral tributes and 800 cards and letters.

Reverend John Caton, rector of St. Mark's officiated at both services. USU President Daryl Chase, LaDell Andersen, and John Cheek also took part. Father McCarthy read the Lord's Prayer before paying tribute to Wayne. "The acceptance of this cross is all the more difficult for the summons came so suddenly and tragically. God called forth Wayne's spirit when his heart was young and his earthly life so promising. Possibly the Book of Wisdom gives us a clue to God's reasoning: 'Being made perfect in a short season while fulfilling a long career; for his soul was pleasing to the Lord; therefore God hastened to bring him to Himself.' We who knew and loved this young man thank God for the privilege of his friendship. We shall all be the better for the example of his loyalty, his great love and respect for his family, his determination to do well in his vocation of daily living, his spirit of good sportsmanship, his love for God and country. Though we are weeping in our loss, we earnestly pray that in his heavenly gain 'he hasn't a tear to shed.' He lived a full cheerful live. He had that rare of God's precious gifts, the joy of seeing every dream in athletics and scholastic supremacy come true."

Wayne Estes: A Hero's Legacy

After the funeral, the hearse took Wayne's body to Sunset Memorial Gardens for burial. The funeral cortege wound fifteen miles to the cemetery. When an extremely low flying plane passed over the hearse carrying the pall bearers, one of his high school friends pretended to shoot it out of the sky. Another remarked, "That's exactly what Wayne would have done." They began reminiscing about the fun times they had had with Wayne. Realizing outsiders might see them laughing, Jim Furaus said, "Can it! Others might not understand our laughter." They became solemn again as the procession wound on.

Tuesday in Logan, the student body held a service for Wayne. Eight days after he had set the records in this packed fieldhouse and received the cheers and adulation from his peers and fans in Cache Valley, the same friends and fans walked into a hushed fieldhouse to pay tribute to the man, not the athlete. School officials had covered the basketball floor, filling it with chairs. As people looked across the fieldhouse, they couldn't see any aisles. Three or four people sat on every step in every aisle. Fire officials would have never allowed that many people in the fieldhouse for an athletic contest, but no one tried to turn people away for this occasion.

President Daryl Chase, in conducting the services, paid tribute to Wayne. "This generation of Aggies will never forget Wayne Estes. We shall remember him, not in the tragedy of his death, but in the many triumphs of his young life. A champion in a hundred ways, he was the handsome youth who taught us dedication to our sciences, arts and crafts; he taught us lessons in humility in times of victory. His fellow students looked to him with pride and attempted to emulate his many virtues. All the faculty would have been proud to call him their son. A rare human being and a cherished friend has departed from our midst."

During the services, Associated Press representative Robert Myers, in a precedent-setting move, presented Coach Andersen with a plaque naming Wayne first-team All-America, the first time an All-America first team member had been named before the end of the

Legacy

regular college season. With that honor, Wayne reached all four goals he set for himself at the beginning of the season. Mr. Myers assured everyone that this didn't come about because of sympathy. With 90 percent of the ballots cast at the time of Wayne's death, they knew he had enough votes to remain in the top five even if no one else voted for him.

Before the benediction, the Utah State concert band and congregation sang the "Alma Mater Hymn." Of his tributes, probably none was as moving or appropriate as this one when thousands, who gave him a standing ovation eight days earlier, with tear-stained eyes tried to sing. By the end of the hymn, no one was singing and many band members couldn't play.

After the services ended, friends, fans, faculty, students, teammates, coaches, young children, and people who never talked personally to Wayne grieved for the unfilled promise of a hero's life. They stood around, almost haunted as they looked over the fieldhouse, hoping to etch his life and legend in their minds. They had lost a friend. Wayne had become a part of their immediate lives, just as their presence at his games became a part of his.

Wayne left a large legacy: To dream, to set goals, to work until those goals were reached, to see value in every individual, a legacy that will be passed on by all who knew him.

SINCE THEN. . . .

At the end of the 1965 basketball season, Utah State University permanently retired Wayne's number, #33. UPI named him first string All-American. The insurance policy Wayne took out the end of January paid the Estes $30,000—triple indemnity because Wayne died accidently within thirty days of signing the policy.

After the 1990-1991 basketball season Wayne still held 15 records at Utah State.

- Most points in a game: 52 against Boston College, Dec. 29, 1964
- Most points in the George Nelson Fieldhouse: 48 against Denver University, Feb. 8, 1965
- Most points in a season: 821 points in 29 games, 1963-64
- Most points in a three-year career: 2,001, 1963-1965
- Most field goals in a game: 21 against Boston College, Dec. 29, 1964
- Most field goals in a season: 309 in 29 games, 1963-64
- Most field goals attempted in a game: 38 against BYU, Feb. 6, 1965
- Most field goals attempted in a season: 645 in 29 games, 1963-64
- Most free throws in a game: 16 against Regis College, Dec. 15, 1962
- Most consecutive free throws: 42 during the 1964-65 season
- Best free throw percentage for a season: .878 1964-1965, 19 games
- Best free throw percentage for a career: .856 1962-65, 75 games
- Most rebounds in a game: 28 against Regis College, Dec. 15, 1962
- Highest scoring average for a season: 33.7 1964-65, 19 games
- Highest scoring average for a career: 26.7 1962-65, 75 games

Wayne Estes: A Hero's Legacy

The importance of these records becomes even more significant when one realizes that Wayne set these records when athletes could only play three years of varsity ball, there was no shot clock, and no three-point fieldgoals. To put it in perspective, Greg Grant (1982-1986) scored 2,175 points in four years while Wayne scored 2,001 points in less than three years. The record for most points in a game in the Spectrum (47) was set by John Coughran of the University of California at Berkeley on Jan. 31, 1971. Wayne still holds the record of most points scored (42) in the University of Montana fieldhouse.

HELEN and JOE ESTES still live in Anaconda. Joe worked at Anaconda Copper for thirty-one years, retiring in 1977. He then worked for the Fish, Wildlife and Parks Department of the state of Montana taking care of two campgrounds near Anaconda every summer for ten years. He underwent open heart surgery in December 1974 and came through it fine. Helen and Joe are very devoted to each other and to Ronnie and his family. They spend as much time as possible at the river during the summer where they fish and enjoy the beauties of nature.

RONNIE ESTES coaches the girls' basketball team and is the school guidance counselor in Phillipsburg, Montana, about forty miles from Anaconda. He and his wife, Molly, have three children: Brad Edward Joseph, 12, Michael Wayne, 8, and Ronnie Joseph Jr., 3. He chose to play baseball in college instead of basketball. He was an outstanding pitcher at the College of Southern Idaho in Twin Falls, Idaho, for two years and then finished at Boise State, in Boise, Idaho.

LADELL ANDERSEN was the head coach at Utah State until 1972. He was named District Coach of the Year four times. He left USU to become the head coach of the Utah Stars, a professional team in the ABA. Before the ABA merged with the NBA, Andersen went back to Utah State to serve as Athletic Director until 1984. He then became the head basketball coach at Brigham Young University, retiring from there in 1989. He now works for the Utah Jazz as a talent scout. He and his wife, Donna, are currently living in St. George, Utah.

Since Then. . . .

JOHN CHEEK retired from coaching at Anaconda High School in 1980 and retired from teaching in 1985. He enjoys his retirement and says he has plenty of time for hunting and fishing and watching his grandchildren.

CHARLES WILLIAMS retired from coaching at Anaconda High School in 1971 and retired from teaching in 1979. He golfs and walks for his exercise. He lives alone in Anaconda since the death of his wife. He spends much time with his three children who all live in Montana.

DEL LYONS married in June 1965. He and Betty have three children: Leslee, 24, Lance, 21, and Leesha, 17. He coached basketball at Roy High in Roy, Utah, for two years and now is a senior account executive with Horace Mann Insurance. He is in good health: playing golf, fishing and enjoying all outdoor athletic activities. They live in Logan, Utah.

JIM FURAUS works in Albuquerque, New Mexico, as an Engineering Management Supervisor. He is still married to Mary Lou after twenty-seven years. They have three children: Mark, 23, Jody, 21, and Jennifer, 16. His kids feel like they know Wayne because they have heard so much about him from both their mom and dad.

TERRY CALE married William DeRohan in August 1974. They live in Boise, Idaho, and have three children: Danielle, 14, David, 13, and Beau, 6. Terry has worked as a flight attendant for United Airlines for the past twenty years and is based out of San Francisco.

PAULA BANDY JORY is a divorced mother of five children: Jana, 22; Jason, 21; Julieanne, 16; Justin, 13; and Jenae, 11. She is a neurolinguistic programmer and teaches self-development seminars in Seattle, Washington. She composes and sings her own music and is also an artist and writer. She loves tennis and other outdoor activities.

JUDY MORSTEIN MARTZ married Harry Martz in 1966. They live in Butte, Montana, with their two children, Justin, 21, and Stacey, 17, and own and operate Martz Disposal Service. She has been heavily involved in community service for a number of years. In 1987 Judy was inducted into the Butte Sports Hall of Fame. She gives motivation speeches and is a field representative for U. S. Senator Conrad Burns.

ESTES' GAME-BY-GAME CAREER SCORING RECORD
SOPHOMORE YEAR--1962-1963

USU	Opponent	(Site)	Score	FGM/FGA	FTM/FTA	RBS	TOTAL
50	Ohio State	(R)	62	4/8	2/2	7	10
80	Butler	(R)	74	6/13	2/3	8	14
79	Montana State	(H)	72	1/10	3/4	7	5
85	Montana State	(H)	67	6/10	4/5	11	16
59	Texas Western	(H)	66	5/15	3/4	7	13
83	Regis (Denver)	(H)	75	9/22	16/17	28	34
101	San Diego State	(H)	57	13/16	6/7	8	32
87	Iowa State	(H)	52	7/17	0/0	13	14
102	Michigan State	(H)	87	9/20	6/6	13	24
75	UCLA	(N)	89	7/19	1/2	9	15
71	Washington	(N)	60	3/8	3/5	8	9
78	Southern Cal	(N)	65	10/23	5/5	8	25
69	Utah	(R)	55	9/20	8/10	11	26
69	Brigham Young	(H)	58	8/16	3/4	11	19
84	Montana	(R)	58	6/10	9/12	9	21
75	Colorado State	(H)	68	5/15	6/7	4	16
88	Denver	(H)	62	8/15	4/6	4	20
70	Brigham Young	(R)	67	9/15	7/8	10	25
97	Utah	(H)	69	10/17	10/11	6	30
85	Montana	(H)	67	9/18	4/4	13	22
55	Texas Western	(R)	57	10/20	4/5	10	24
78	New Mexico	(R)	48	6/13	3/3	3	15
65	Air Force	(R)	66	12/20	2/2	10	26
74	Denver	(R)	70	7/19	4/5	10	18
69	Creighton	(H)	68	8/16	2/5	15	18
60	Colorado State	(R)	67	6/11	4/4	4	16
75	Arizona State	(N)	79	12/22	8/8	9	32
	TOTALS			205/428	129/154	256	539
				.479	.838	9.5	20.0

JUNIOR YEAR--1963-1964

USU	Opponent	(Site)	Score	FGM/FGA	FTM/FTA	RBS	TOTAL
97	Loyala	(H)	85	12/18	13/14	19	37
102	Fresno	(H)	71	3/8	3/4	9	9*
94	Texas A & M	(H)	68	16/24	9/11	5	41
91	Creighton	(R)	96	9/20	3/3	14	21
68	Iowa State	(R)	77	11/29	3/3	6	25
115	New Mexico State	(H)	75	15/26	5/8	17	35
64	Arizona	(H)	60	11/25	5/5	16	27
95	Bradley	(H)	90	6/20	4/4	10	16
79	Ohio State	(H)	66	14/23	12/14	21	40
84	Utah	(H)	72	9/19	10/11	15	28
83	Air Force Academy	(H)	73	7/13	11/13	14	25
99	Montana	(R)	70	15/23	12/13	15	42
85	Colorado State	(H)	70	12/25	5/8	16	29
105	Brigham Young	(H)	90	9/18	10/10	17	28
90	Brigham Young	(R)	73	10/31	5/5	10	25
67	Utah	(R)	79	6/20	15/17	12	27
75	Denver	(H)	56	14/25	0/1	20	28
77	Montana State	(R)	73	10/16	9/13	14	29
88	Montana State	(R)	80	12/21	9/9	11	33
85	Colorado State	(R)	84	14/24	7/10	25	35
74	Denver	(R)	72	10/17	6/7	4	26
94	Seattle	(H)	96	10/34	5/6	11	25
103	Montana	(H)	81	8/16	5/6	12	21
85	LaSalle	(R)	90	8/22	7/10	10	23
125	American U	(R)	100	18/32	6/6	12	42
75	Providence	(R)	85	14/30	3/4	17	31
92	Arizona State	(N)	90	14/29	10/11	8	38
58	San Francisco	(N)	64	6/19	9/9	11	21
78	Seattle	(N)	80	6/18	2/3	6	14
	TOTALS			309/645	203/238	377	821
				.479	.853	13.0	28.3

*Wayne played less than half a game because he sprained his ankle in the first half.

SENIOR YEAR--1964-1965

USU	Opponent	(Site)	Score	FGM/FGA	FTM/FTA	RBS	TOTAL
107	Idaho State	(H)	66	14/27	7/7	14	35
88	Butler	(H)	84	15/37	3/4	15	33
96	Loyola Calif	(H)	69	14/26	9/9	21	37
98	U of Pacific	(H)	74	11/24	7/7	25	29
101	Nevada	(H)	80	16/32	8/8	16	40
69	Bradley	(R)	75	13/29	2/2	11	28
69	Minnesota	(R)	88	11/28	5/5	9	27
86	San Jose State	(H)	73	10/21	13/14	14	33
71	San Francisco	(R)	86	6/15	7/8	9	19
98	Arizona State	(N)	96	13/26	2/4	9	28
118	Boston College	(N)	120	21/34	10/14	16	52
86	Utah	(R)	84	12/24	8/8	13	32
90	Brigham Young	(H)	99	13/30	8/8	13	34
78	Colorado State	(H)	89	11/20	9/14	19	31
62	Texas Western	(R)	68	11/15	4/5	8	26
93	Arizona State	(R)	99	10/25	9/10	12	29
104	Utah	(H)	111	17/37	9/10	14	43
80	Brigham Young	(R)	89	14/38	9/9	8	37
91	Denver	(H)	69	20/30	8/10	14	48
	TOTALS			252/518	137/156	260	641
				.486	.878	13.7	33.7

*Wayne scored 42 points (16 fieldgoals and 10/12 free throws) against a US Marine team in the first game of the Hawaii Tournament, but because they are not in the NCAA, those statistics didn't count in his totals.

CAREER TOTALS

	FGM/FGA	FTM/FTA	REBOUNDS	TOTAL POINTS
SOPHOMORE YEAR	205/428	129/154	256	539
	.479	.838	9.5	20.0
JUNIOR YEAR	309/654	203/238	377	821
	.479	.853	13.0	28.3
SENIOR YEAR	252/518	137/156	260	641
	.486	.878	13.7	33.7
TOTALS	766/1600	469/548	893	2001
	.479	.856	11.9	26.7

ABOUT THE AUTHOR

Eleanor Olson was born in Pocatello, Idaho but moved to Ogden one month later. She considers herself an Ogden native as this is the only place she has ever called home. She graduated with her B. S. Degree from Utah State University in 1966 and received an M. S. Degree in English with a writing emphasis in 1988 from the same institution. As a freshman winter quarter, she attended every home basketball game. Wayne, a sophomore, impressed her with his strength and gentleness on and off the court. She met him spring quarter that year. She continued to follow his collegiate career for the next two years. They became friends because she was the sports editor of the *Buzzer* (USU's yearbook). She wrote the 1965 yearbook eulogy for Wayne.

She has taught English at Roy High School, in Roy, Utah, for the past twenty-five years. The school and her students have become her second home and family. She has worked as a Senior Class Advisor, English Department Head besides being the official scorekeeper for the boys' basketball and baseball teams.

She has always loved watching sports. As a youngster, she attended many minor league baseball games with her parents at John Affleck Park in Ogden. She saved newspaper clipping on the Brooklyn Dodgers, the Los Angles Lakers, and the Baltimore Colts while in elementary and junior high school. In high school, she saved her lunch money to attend away football and basketball games. She has also coached boys' basketball teams in the Roy Recreation League.

ORDER FORM

Please send me _____ copies of WAYNE ESTES: A HERO'S LEGACY at $6.00 per copy, for which I enclose check or money order for _____. Add $1.50 for postage and handling per book. Make checks payable to and order from: Olson Publishing, P. O. Box 1302, Ogden, Utah, 84402.

Name: _____

Street or Box: _____

City, State, Zip: _____